Written Calculation Teacher's Resource Book

Hilary Koll and Steve Mills

Schofield & Sims

Published by Schofield & Sims Ltd, Dogley Mill, Fenay Bridge, Huddersfield HD8 0NQ, UK Tel 01484 607080 www.schofieldandsims.co.uk
First published in 2015. Copyright © Schofield & Sims Ltd, 2015.

Authors: Hilary Koll and Steve Mills

Hilary Koll and Steve Mills have asserted their moral rights under the Copyright, Designs and Patents Act, 1988, to be identified as the authors of this work.

British Library Cataloguing in Publication Data
A catalogue record for this book is available from the British Library.

All rights reserved. Except where otherwise indicated no part of this publication may be reproduced, stored in a retrieval system, or transmitted in any form or by any means, electronic, mechanical, photocopying, recording or otherwise, without either the prior permission of the publisher or a licence permitting restricted copying in the United Kingdom issued by the Copyright Licensing Agency Limited, Saffron House, 6–10 Kirby Street, London EC1N 8TS.

Commissioned by **Carolyn Richardson Publishing Services (www.publiserve.co.uk)**

Design by **Ledgard Jepson Ltd**
Cover illustration by **Joe Hance (joehance.co.uk)**
Printed in the UK by **Wyndeham Gait Ltd, Grimsby, Lincolnshire**
ISBN 978 07217 1300 7

Contents

Introduction	4
Purpose and benefits	4
Prerequisites for working on Written Calculation	4
Linking written methods of calculation and place value	4
The importance of estimating and checking	5
Extension	5
Getting the most out of the Teacher's Resource Book	5
Teacher's Guide	5
Free downloads	5
Addition: Further practice questions	6
Steps 1 to 2	6
Steps 3 to 4	7
Steps 5 to 6	8
Steps 7 to 8	9
Steps 9 to 10	10
Steps 11 to 12	11
Steps 13 to 14	12
Steps 15 to 16	13
Steps 17 to 18	14
Addition: Problem solving questions	15
Subtraction: Further practice questions	16
Steps 1 to 2	16
Steps 3 to 4	17
Steps 5 to 6	18
Steps 7 to 8	19
Steps 9 to 10	20
Steps 11 to 12	21
Steps 13 to 14	22
Steps 15 to 16	23
Steps 17 to 18	24
Subtraction: Problem solving questions	25
Multiplication 1: Further practice questions	26
Steps 1 to 2	26
Steps 3 to 4	27
Steps 5 to 6	28
Steps 7 to 8	29
Steps 9 to 10	30
Steps 11 to 12	31
Steps 13 to 14	32
Steps 15 to 16	33
Steps 17 to 18	34

Multiplication 1: Problem solving questions	35
Multiplication 2: Further practice questions	36
Steps 1 to 2	36
Steps 3 to 4	37
Steps 5 to 6	38
Steps 7 to 8	39
Steps 9 to 10	40
Steps 11 to 12	41
Steps 13 to 14	42
Steps 15 to 16	43
Steps 17 to 18	44
Multiplication 2: Problem solving questions	45
Division 1: Further practice questions	46
Steps 1 to 2	46
Steps 3 to 4	47
Steps 5 to 6	48
Steps 7 to 8	49
Steps 9 to 10	50
Steps 11 to 12	51
Steps 13 to 14	52
Steps 15 to 16	53
Steps 17 to 18	54
Division 1: Problem solving questions	55
Division 2: Further practice questions	56
Steps 1 to 2	56
Steps 3 to 4	57
Steps 5 to 6	58
Steps 7 to 8	59
Steps 9 to 10	60
Steps 11 to 12	61
Steps 13 to 14	62
Steps 15 to 16	63
Steps 17 to 18	64
Division 2: Problem solving questions	65
Answers	67
Addition	68
Subtraction	70
Multiplication 1	72
Multiplication 2	74
Division 1	76
Division 2	78

Schofield & Sims | Written Calculation: Teacher's Resource Book

Introduction

Schofield & Sims Written Calculation provides carefully graded practice in the aspects of written calculation that pupils need to master by the end of Key Stage 2. It equips you, the teacher, with all you need to explain, demonstrate and teach written addition, subtraction, multiplication and division. **Written Calculation** is primarily for Key Stage 2 pupils but may also be suitable for some older pupils.

The series comprises six **Pupil Books** with accompanying **Answer Books**, plus this **Teacher's Resource Book** and a **Teacher's Guide** – both of which cover the whole series.

The questions included in each Pupil Book incorporate a range of mathematical learning objectives from the National Curriculum 2014. These questions require pupils to apply their knowledge of place value, number facts and problem solving as well as written calculation and mathematical operations. Progression through each book provides opportunities to practise these skills, further developing pupils' conceptual understanding and fluency in maths.

Purpose and benefits

Written Calculation provides simple instruction, worked examples and structured practice in all four of the key mathematical operations. It is designed for regular classroom use alongside your existing maths lessons. As pupils progress through Key Stage 2, gradually developing their maths skills, they are also likely to change teachers on an annual basis. This series provides stability and continuity, ensuring that none of the vital steps are missed as pupils learn to apply their skills while moving up through the school. For this reason, you may wish to use **Written Calculation** as the basis of a whole-school approach to written calculation.

Further benefits of using **Written Calculation** on a regular basis include:

- preparation and good practice for national tests
- support for work in other areas of the primary and secondary curriculum
- preparation for using written calculation proficiently on a day-to-day basis in future education, in the workplace and in everyday life.

Prerequisites for working on Written Calculation

Pupils who have not yet memorised number bonds may find it useful temporarily to refer to a list of number bonds, which are downloadable from the **Written Calculation** pages of the Schofield & Sims website. This will allow them to focus on the procedures of the written method. Once pupils are familiar with these facts, they will no longer need the list. Where an operation is covered by two books, as is the case for multiplication and division, pupils should work through the first book before beginning the second. Prerequisites specific to individual books are given in the teaching notes of the accompanying Teacher's Guide. Each of the six Pupil Books provides pupils with 18 'steps' of learning. Pupils should work through the steps consecutively to ensure that they master key ideas.

Linking written methods of calculation and place value

The steps in **Written Calculation** demonstrate to pupils the process of written column methods and provide them with the necessary structured practice. In order to derive the maximum benefit, it is important that pupils have a good understanding of place value. You can enhance pupils' understanding of why and how each process works by drawing links between the methods they are learning and place value concepts. The accompanying Teacher's Guide provides key teaching notes plus expanded representations of the written methods to support you.

The importance of estimating and checking

It is essential to remind pupils of the importance of checking their answers to see if they are sensible. As they progress, ask pupils to check each answer with an inverse calculation: for example, check a written subtraction with a written addition calculation. As pupils' confidence in a written method grows, encourage them instead to make estimates before they begin each calculation.

Extension

The final steps in each Pupil Book extend more able pupils and address more difficult aspects of written calculation, including giving decimal answers. They may be used at your discretion to stretch those pupils who have already mastered the basics and corresponding *Further practice questions* and *Problem solving questions* are included within this Teacher's Resource Book.

Getting the most out of the Teacher's Resource Book

This Teacher's Resource Book provides additional questions, corresponding to the steps in each of the Pupil Books. These photocopiable resources supplement the material contained in each Pupil Book and may be used for further practice, revision or homework, as pupils reach the final stages of a book. Answers are provided at the back of this book and pupils will need spare squared paper for working. The resources align to the National Curriculum learning requirements, as outlined in the **Written Calculation** Teacher's Guide. The resources in this Teacher's Resource Book include the following.

- *Further practice questions* provide up to ten questions per step, corresponding to the steps in the Pupil Books. Each page comprises questions covering two steps. You may wish to photocopy the whole page for pupils to work through or you may prefer to use the dotted lines and cut out the questions that correspond to a specific step in order to stick them into an exercise or homework book.

- *Problem solving questions* provide additional word problems, similar to those appearing in the *Problem solving* section of each step in the Pupil Books. Each page comprises 12 questions per book and encourages children to apply written calculation methods to solve a variety of practical problems.

Teacher's Guide

The accompanying Teacher's Guide helps you to integrate the series within a whole-school approach to written calculation. The useful teaching notes and ideas for planning lessons give detailed explanations of each step for addition, subtraction, multiplication and division. The Teacher's Guide also includes two photocopiable *Assessment tests* per topic, covering the same areas as the work provided in the Pupil Books (one question per step). A *Mixed calculations test* gives pupils practice in deciding which operation to use for a variety of different word problems.

Free downloads

Further resources are available for download from the **Written Calculation** pages of the Schofield & Sims website. These resources include, for example, lists of number bonds, a multiplication square and division facts, which some pupils may need to support their earliest steps in **Written Calculation**. The selection of downloads available is updated regularly to meet your changing requirements and the demands of the National Curriculum.

Written Calculation — Addition

Further practice questions: Steps 1 to 2

Name: _____

Class/Set: _____ Date: _____

Using squared paper for working, work out your answer to each question.
Then write your answer on the line next to the question.

Step 1

1 24 + 63 = _____

2 36 + 42 = _____

3 43 + 55 = _____

4 27 + 61 = _____

5 33 + 66 = _____

6 44 + 45 = _____

7 61 + 15 = _____

8 72 + 17 = _____

9 32 + 62 = _____

10 64 + 24 = _____

Step 2

1 344 + 545 = _____

2 671 + 215 = _____

3 234 + 163 = _____

4 326 + 342 = _____

5 431 + 565 = _____

6 273 + 614 = _____

7 721 + 174 = _____

8 323 + 676 = _____

9 302 + 682 = _____

10 693 + 204 = _____

From: **Written Calculation: Teacher's Resource Book** by Hilary Koll and Steve Mills (ISBN 978 07217 1300 7). Copyright © Schofield & Sims Ltd, 2015. Published by Schofield & Sims Ltd, Dogley Mill, Fenay Bridge, Huddersfield HD8 0NQ, UK (www.schofieldandsims.co.uk). This page may be photocopied after purchase for use within your school or institution only.

Written Calculation — **Addition**

Further practice questions: Steps 3 to 4

Name: _____

Class/Set: _____ Date: _____

Using squared paper for working, work out your answer to each question.
Then write your answer on the line next to the question.

Step 3

1. 238 + 153 = _____
2. 324 + 347 = _____
3. 326 + 666 = _____
4. 725 + 137 = _____
5. 309 + 682 = _____
6. 646 + 204 = _____
7. 436 + 535 = _____
8. 279 + 614 = _____
9. 325 + 545 = _____
10. 678 + 218 = _____

Step 4

1. 383 + 532 = _____
2. 245 + 471 = _____
3. 266 + 662 = _____
4. 254 + 374 = _____
5. 491 + 372 = _____
6. 463 + 284 = _____
7. 361 + 357 = _____
8. 692 + 147 = _____
9. 253 + 465 = _____
10. 784 + 185 = _____

From: **Written Calculation: Teacher's Resource Book** by Hilary Koll and Steve Mills (ISBN 978 07217 1300 7). Copyright © Schofield & Sims Ltd, 2015. Published by Schofield & Sims Ltd, Dogley Mill, Fenay Bridge, Huddersfield HD8 0NQ, UK (www.schofieldandsims.co.uk). This page may be photocopied after purchase for use within your school or institution only.

Written Calculation — Addition

Further practice questions: Steps 5 to 6

Name: _____

Class/Set: _____ Date: _____

Using squared paper for working, work out your answer to each question.
Then write your answer on the line next to the question.

Step 5

1. 623 + 539 = _____
2. 845 + 471 = _____
3. 366 + 962 = _____
4. 628 + 657 = _____
5. 602 + 748 = _____
6. 853 + 464 = _____
7. 954 + 338 = _____
8. 591 + 572 = _____
9. 863 + 884 = _____
10. 777 + 718 = _____

Step 6

1. 323 + 514 + 124 = _____
2. 242 + 471 + 213 = _____
3. 628 + 617 + 238 = _____
4. 692 + 741 + 334 = _____
5. 853 + 461 + 250 = _____
6. 321 + 317 + 218 = _____
7. 619 + 128 + 409 = _____
8. 553 + 465 + 651 = _____
9. 782 + 185 + 382 = _____
10. 566 + 782 + 671 = _____

From: **Written Calculation: Teacher's Resource Book** by Hilary Koll and Steve Mills (ISBN 978 07217 1300 7). Copyright © Schofield & Sims Ltd, 2015. Published by Schofield & Sims Ltd, Dogley Mill, Fenay Bridge, Huddersfield HD8 0NQ, UK (www.schofieldandsims.co.uk). This page may be photocopied after purchase for use within your school or institution only.

Written Calculation — Addition

Further practice questions: Steps 7 to 8

Name: _____

Class/Set: _____   Date: _____

Using squared paper for working, work out your answer to each question.
Then write your answer on the line next to the question.

Step 7

1. 3216 + 3118 = _____
2. 4319 + 1810 = _____
3. 5523 + 2651 = _____
4. 5382 + 1382 = _____
5. 4666 + 4271 = _____
6. 3423 + 5724 = _____
7. 2452 + 4271 = _____
8. 6283 + 1156 = _____
9. 5492 + 3434 = _____
10. 8553 + 1352 = _____

Step 8

1. 379 + 255 = _____
2. 527 + 277 = _____
3. 216 + 195 = _____
4. 455 + 277 = _____
5. 386 + 386 = _____
6. 498 + 434 = _____
7. 553 + 758 = _____
8. 666 + 177 = _____
9. 723 + 588 = _____
10. 885 + 156 = _____

From: **Written Calculation: Teacher's Resource Book** by Hilary Koll and Steve Mills (ISBN 978 07217 1300 7). Copyright © Schofield & Sims Ltd, 2015. Published by Schofield & Sims Ltd, Dogley Mill, Fenay Bridge, Huddersfield HD8 0NQ, UK (www.schofieldandsims.co.uk). This page may be photocopied after purchase for use within your school or institution only.

Written Calculation — **Addition**

Further practice questions: Steps 9 to 10

Name: _____

Class/Set: _____   Date: _____

Using squared paper for working, work out your answer to each question.
Then write your answer on the line next to the question.

Step 9

1. 4319 + 1415 = _____
2. 5527 + 2657 = _____
3. 3216 + 3918 = _____
4. 2455 + 4277 = _____
5. 5386 + 1386 = _____
6. 5438 + 3434 = _____
7. 6553 + 1752 = _____
8. 4666 + 4571 = _____
9. 3423 + 5728 = _____
10. 6285 + 1156 = _____

Step 10

1. 9527 + 657 = _____
2. 9319 + 915 = _____
3. 3216 + 7118 = _____
4. 7386 + 8176 = _____
5. 8455 + 6277 = _____
6. 9838 + 334 = _____
7. 9553 + 752 = _____
8. 9666 + 571 = _____
9. 9425 + 7128 = _____
10. 6285 + 8156 = _____

From: **Written Calculation: Teacher's Resource Book** by Hilary Koll and Steve Mills (ISBN 978 07217 1300 7). Copyright © Schofield & Sims Ltd, 2015. Published by Schofield & Sims Ltd, Dogley Mill, Fenay Bridge, Huddersfield HD8 0NQ, UK (www.schofieldandsims.co.uk). This page may be photocopied after purchase for use within your school or institution only.

Written Calculation — Addition

Further practice questions: Steps 11 to 12

Name: _____

Class/Set: _____   Date: _____

Using squared paper for working, work out your answer to each question.
Then write your answer on the line next to the question.

Step 11

1. 4319 + 6895 = _____
2. 7386 + 8676 = _____
3. 9838 + 3584 = _____
4. 3216 + 7788 = _____
5. 8455 + 6677 = _____
6. 5527 + 6597 = _____
7. 3553 + 7569 = _____
8. 8425 + 7988 = _____
9. 6585 + 8556 = _____
10. 7666 + 5766 = _____

Step 12

1. 7325 + 6139 + 3786 = _____
2. 4319 + 1734 + 1545 = _____
3. 7353 + 6845 + 4444 = _____
4. 9335 + 4195 + 677 = _____
5. 7666 + 644 + 5846 = _____
6. 8327 + 6335 + 5867 = _____
7. 6585 + 3231 + 8556 = _____
8. 7342 + 6191 + 338 = _____
9. 3553 + 134 + 7569 = _____
10. 8425 + 195 + 7932 = _____

From: **Written Calculation: Teacher's Resource Book** by Hilary Koll and Steve Mills (ISBN 978 07217 1300 7). Copyright © Schofield & Sims Ltd, 2015. Published by Schofield & Sims Ltd, Dogley Mill, Fenay Bridge, Huddersfield HD8 0NQ, UK (www.schofieldandsims.co.uk). This page may be photocopied after purchase for use within your school or institution only.

Written Calculation — Addition

Further practice questions: Steps 13 to 14

Name: _____

Class/Set: _____ Date: _____

Using squared paper for working, work out your answer to each question.
Then write your answer on the line next to the question.

Step 13

1 38 358 + 35 384 = _____

2 73 586 + 86 776 = _____

3 32 165 + 77 828 = _____

4 84 565 + 66 717 = _____

5 44 319 + 61 695 = _____

6 55 247 + 65 297 = _____

7 76 646 + 57 266 = _____

8 35 534 + 75 659 = _____

9 84 225 + 79 848 = _____

10 65 865 + 85 536 = _____

Step 14

Find the totals.

1 32 319 + 582 + 7386 + 8676 + 462 = _____

2 3238 + 2584 + 474 + 32 216 + 788 = _____

3 855 + 66 277 + 5526 + 353 + 6597 = _____

4 13 553 + 7569 + 425 + 7988 + 364 = _____

5 6585 + 81 556 + 375 + 766 + 5766 = _____

From: **Written Calculation: Teacher's Resource Book** by Hilary Koll and Steve Mills (ISBN 978 07217 1300 7). Copyright © Schofield & Sims Ltd, 2015. Published by Schofield & Sims Ltd, Dogley Mill, Fenay Bridge, Huddersfield HD8 0NQ, UK (www.schofieldandsims.co.uk). This page may be photocopied after purchase for use within your school or institution only.

Written Calculation — Addition

Further practice questions: Steps 15 to 16

Name: _____

Class/Set: _____   Date: _____

Using squared paper for working, work out your answer to each question.
Then write your answer on the line next to the question.

Step 15

1 Two hundred and sixteen thousand and thirty-two plus three hundred and seventy-two thousand and sixty-one.

_____

2 Five hundred and six thousand and forty-nine plus seven hundred and eleven thousand and fifty-five.

_____

3 Six hundred and forty thousand, two hundred and four plus five hundred and eleven thousand and seven.

_____

Step 16

1 37.9 + 25.5 = _____

2 52.7 + 27.7 = _____

3 21.6 + 19.5 = _____

4 114.5 + 27.7 = _____

5 238.6 + 38.6 = _____

6 49.8 + 43.4 = _____

7 55.3 + 705.8 = _____

8 66.6 + 317.7 = _____

9 722.3 + 528.8 = _____

10 868.5 + 155.6 = _____

Written Calculation — Addition

Further practice questions: Steps 17 to 18

Name: _____

Class/Set: _____ Date: _____

Using squared paper for working, work out your answer to each question.
Then write your answer on the line next to the question.

Step 17

1. 443.19 + 66.95 = _____

2. 735.86 + 87.76 = _____

3. 98.35 + 353.84 = _____

4. 316.57 + 778.28 = _____

5. 84.55 + 667.17 = _____

6. 552.47 + 652.97 = _____

7. 355.34 + 756.59 = _____

8. 84.25 + 768.48 = _____

9. 648.65 + 85.36 = _____

10. 763.46 + 52.66 = _____

Step 18

1. 524.7 + 62.97 = _____

2. 355.34 + 5.9 = _____

3. 82.25 + 798.4 = _____

4. 658.65 + 5.536 = _____

5. 44.319 + 6.95 = _____

6. 73.586 + 7.76 = _____

7. 83.58 + 338.4 = _____

8. 321.65 + 77.828 = _____

9. 86.5 + 66.717 = _____

10. 764.6 + 2.66 = _____

From: **Written Calculation: Teacher's Resource Book** by Hilary Koll and Steve Mills (ISBN 978 07217 1300 7). Copyright © Schofield & Sims Ltd, 2015. Published by Schofield & Sims Ltd, Dogley Mill, Fenay Bridge, Huddersfield HD8 0NQ, UK (www.schofieldandsims.co.uk). This page may be photocopied after purchase for use within your school or institution only.

Written Calculation — Addition

Problem solving questions

Name: _____

Class/Set: _____ Date: _____

Using squared paper for working, work out your answer to each question.
Then write your answer on the line next to the question.

1 What is the total of 458 and 237? _____

2 Paul has a pedometer that tells him how many steps he takes each day. On Monday he takes 4385 steps. On Tuesday he takes 1273 more steps than on Monday. How many steps does he take on Tuesday? _____

3 A TV that cost £1257 is increased in price by £186. What is the new price? _____

4 Find the sum of 465, 452 and 251. _____

5 Which year is 756 years after 1247 AD? _____

6 Ahmed scored 8953 points in the first round of a computer game and 2745 in the second round. What was his total score? _____

7 A forestry service planted 50 687 trees last year and 43 754 this year. How many did they plant altogether? _____

8 5867 more planes landed at an airport in June than in March, when 3857 planes landed there. How many planes landed there in June? _____

9 Amy's first throw of the ball went 28.4m. Her second throw went 12.7m further. How far did her second throw go? _____

10 How much did Kim pay in total for items costing £14.57 and £45.86? _____

11 Add 80.82 to 802.8. _____

12 The first prize in a tennis tournament is six hundred thousand and eighty-nine pounds. The second prize is seventy-two thousand, four hundred and forty pounds. How much are the two prizes altogether? _____

From: **Written Calculation: Teacher's Resource Book** by Hilary Koll and Steve Mills (ISBN 978 07217 1300 7). Copyright © Schofield & Sims Ltd, 2015. Published by Schofield & Sims Ltd, Dogley Mill, Fenay Bridge, Huddersfield HD8 0NQ, UK (www.schofieldandsims.co.uk). This page may be photocopied after purchase for use within your school or institution only.

Written Calculation   **Subtraction**

Further practice questions: Steps 1 to 2

Name: _____

Class/Set: _____ Date: _____

Using squared paper for working, work out your answer to each question.
Then write your answer on the line next to the question.

Step 1

1 98 – 63 = _____

2 85 – 42 = _____

3 66 – 55 = _____

4 96 – 61 = _____

5 87 – 66 = _____

6 73 – 42 = _____

7 69 – 15 = _____

8 78 – 17 = _____

9 94 – 62 = _____

10 65 – 24 = _____

Step 2

1 869 – 545 = _____

2 437 – 215 = _____

3 575 – 163 = _____

4 657 – 342 = _____

5 699 – 565 = _____

6 925 – 614 = _____

7 793 – 172 = _____

8 798 – 676 = _____

9 826 – 602 = _____

10 697 – 204 = _____

From: **Written Calculation: Teacher's Resource Book** by Hilary Koll and Steve Mills (ISBN 978 07217 1300 7). Copyright © Schofield & Sims Ltd, 2015. Published by Schofield & Sims Ltd, Dogley Mill, Fenay Bridge, Huddersfield HD8 0NQ, UK (www.schofieldandsims.co.uk). This page may be photocopied after purchase for use within your school or institution only.

Written Calculation — Subtraction

Further practice questions: Steps 3 to 4

Name: _____

Class/Set: _____ Date: _____

Using squared paper for working, work out your answer to each question. Then write your answer on the line next to the question.

Step 3

1. 281 − 153 = _____
2. 694 − 347 = _____
3. 793 − 666 = _____
4. 765 − 137 = _____
5. 891 − 642 = _____
6. 441 − 204 = _____
7. 882 − 535 = _____
8. 971 − 614 = _____
9. 665 − 548 = _____
10. 677 − 218 = _____

Step 4

1. 723 − 532 = _____
2. 845 − 471 = _____
3. 966 − 682 = _____
4. 654 − 374 = _____
5. 888 − 392 = _____
6. 447 − 284 = _____
7. 728 − 357 = _____
8. 639 − 147 = _____
9. 818 − 465 = _____
10. 946 − 185 = _____

From: **Written Calculation: Teacher's Resource Book** by Hilary Koll and Steve Mills (ISBN 978 07217 1300 7). Copyright © Schofield & Sims Ltd, 2015. Published by Schofield & Sims Ltd, Dogley Mill, Fenay Bridge, Huddersfield HD8 0NQ, UK (www.schofieldandsims.co.uk). This page may be photocopied after purchase for use within your school or institution only.

Written Calculation — Subtraction

Further practice questions: Steps 5 to 6

Name: _____

Class/Set: _____ Date: _____

Using squared paper for working, work out your answer to each question.
Then write your answer on the line next to the question.

Step 5

1. 628 − 531 = _____

2. 845 − 471 = _____

3. 571 − 262 = _____

4. 884 − 657 = _____

5. 992 − 748 = _____

6. 857 − 464 = _____

7. 954 − 338 = _____

8. 815 − 142 = _____

9. 863 − 256 = _____

10. 777 − 618 = _____

Step 6

1. 3178 − 1254 = _____

2. 4319 − 1415 = _____

3. 5597 − 2657 = _____

4. 7216 − 3911 = _____

5. 8498 − 4717 = _____

6. 5386 − 1784 = _____

7. 8432 − 3831 = _____

8. 6253 − 1752 = _____

9. 7166 − 4531 = _____

10. 9429 − 5728 = _____

From: **Written Calculation: Teacher's Resource Book** by Hilary Koll and Steve Mills (ISBN 978 07217 1300 7). Copyright © Schofield & Sims Ltd, 2015. Published by Schofield & Sims Ltd, Dogley Mill, Fenay Bridge, Huddersfield HD8 0NQ, UK (www.schofieldandsims.co.uk). This page may be photocopied after purchase for use within your school or institution only.

Written Calculation — Subtraction

Further practice questions: Steps 7 to 8

Name: _____

Class/Set: _____ Date: _____

Using squared paper for working, work out your answer to each question.
Then write your answer on the line next to the question.

Step 7

1. 7286 – 3518 = _____
2. 4364 – 1818 = _____
3. 5521 – 2703 = _____
4. 5382 – 1658 = _____
5. 8666 – 4718 = _____
6. 9483 – 5724 = _____
7. 7452 – 4713 = _____
8. 6283 – 1756 = _____
9. 5492 – 3738 = _____
10. 8553 – 2846 = _____

Step 8

1. 823 – 255 = _____
2. 553 – 277 = _____
3. 614 – 145 = _____
4. 455 – 257 = _____
5. 734 – 386 = _____
6. 912 – 434 = _____
7. 947 – 758 = _____
8. 666 – 177 = _____
9. 723 – 588 = _____
10. 855 – 156 = _____

From: **Written Calculation: Teacher's Resource Book** by Hilary Koll and Steve Mills (ISBN 978 07217 1300 7). Copyright © Schofield & Sims Ltd, 2015. Published by Schofield & Sims Ltd, Dogley Mill, Fenay Bridge, Huddersfield HD8 0NQ, UK (www.schofieldandsims.co.uk). This page may be photocopied after purchase for use within your school or institution only.

Written Calculation — Subtraction

Further practice questions: Steps 9 to 10

Name: _____

Class/Set: _____   Date: _____

Using squared paper for working, work out your answer to each question. Then write your answer on the line next to the question.

Step 9

1. 4319 − 1485 = _____
2. 5923 − 2657 = _____
3. 8216 − 3971 = _____
4. 7458 − 4477 = _____
5. 5226 − 1386 = _____
6. 5438 − 3379 = _____
7. 6553 − 1782 = _____
8. 7666 − 4971 = _____
9. 6423 − 5258 = _____
10. 4546 − 1873 = _____

Step 10

1. 7401 − 5368 = _____
2. 9805 − 2497 = _____
3. 6059 − 3275 = _____
4. 8047 − 4573 = _____
5. 5603 − 1486 = _____
6. 8034 − 5983 = _____
7. 8026 − 4766 = _____
8. 7058 − 3276 = _____
9. 6305 − 2128 = _____
10. 6036 − 1865 = _____

From: **Written Calculation: Teacher's Resource Book** by Hilary Koll and Steve Mills (ISBN 978 07217 1300 7). Copyright © Schofield & Sims Ltd, 2015. Published by Schofield & Sims Ltd, Dogley Mill, Fenay Bridge, Huddersfield HD8 0NQ, UK (www.schofieldandsims.co.uk). This page may be photocopied after purchase for use within your school or institution only.

Written Calculation — Subtraction

Further practice questions: Steps 11 to 12

Name: _____

Class/Set: _____ Date: _____

Using squared paper for working, work out your answer to each question.
Then write your answer on the line next to the question.

Step 11

1. 43 873 – 15 225 = _____
2. 85 629 – 17 346 = _____
3. 52 817 – 48 372 = _____
4. 88 391 – 74 473 = _____
5. 68 232 – 15 819 = _____
6. 82 612 – 67 308 = _____
7. 96 375 – 75 969 = _____
8. 95 959 – 59 595 = _____
9. 72 520 – 14 216 = _____
10. 56 748 – 28 457 = _____

Step 12

1. 59 628 – 32 963 = _____
2. 99 720 – 43 346 = _____
3. 47 508 – 21 833 = _____
4. 84 358 – 46 722 = _____
5. 54 437 – 12 763 = _____
6. 87 842 – 64 377 = _____
7. 68 067 – 5682 = _____
8. 64 428 – 2774 = _____
9. 86 948 – 46 669 = _____
10. 67 226 – 25 873 = _____

From: **Written Calculation: Teacher's Resource Book** by Hilary Koll and Steve Mills (ISBN 978 07217 1300 7). Copyright © Schofield & Sims Ltd, 2015. Published by Schofield & Sims Ltd, Dogley Mill, Fenay Bridge, Huddersfield HD8 0NQ, UK (www.schofieldandsims.co.uk). This page may be photocopied after purchase for use within your school or institution only.

Written Calculation — Subtraction

Further practice questions: Steps 13 to 14

Name: _____

Class/Set: _____ Date: _____

Using squared paper for working, work out your answer to each question.
Then write your answer on the line next to the question.

Step 13

1. 27 058 – 13 276 = _____

2. 66 305 – 42 128 = _____

3. 67 401 – 25 368 = _____

4. 79 805 – 32 497 = _____

5. 78 047 – 44 573 = _____

6. 80 603 – 31 486 = _____

7. 46 059 – 13 275 = _____

8. 56 036 – 21 865 = _____

9. 68 034 – 35 983 = _____

10. 78 026 – 14 766 = _____

Step 14

1. 82 433 – 37 564 = _____

2. 46 224 – 13 565 = _____

3. 52 311 – 21 865 = _____

4. 63 425 – 35 886 = _____

5. 78 111 – 14 766 = _____

6. 68 520 – 48 737 = _____

7. 63 542 – 47 869 = _____

8. 63 559 – 29 868 = _____

9. 79 231 – 32 497 = _____

10. 73 525 – 46 657 = _____

From: **Written Calculation: Teacher's Resource Book** by Hilary Koll and Steve Mills (ISBN 978 07217 1300 7). Copyright © Schofield & Sims Ltd, 2015. Published by Schofield & Sims Ltd, Dogley Mill, Fenay Bridge, Huddersfield HD8 0NQ, UK (www.schofieldandsims.co.uk). This page may be photocopied after purchase for use within your school or institution only.

Written Calculation — Subtraction

Further practice questions: Steps 15 to 16

Name: _____

Class/Set: _____ Date: _____

Using squared paper for working, work out your answer to each question.
Then write your answer on the line next to the question.

Step 15

1. 82 003 − 37 564 = _____

2. 40 024 − 13 565 = _____

3. 50 007 − 21 869 = _____

4. 63 005 − 35 886 = _____

5. 70 061 − 14 766 = _____

6. 68 002 − 48 737 = _____

7. 60 002 − 47 869 = _____

8. 60 029 − 29 868 = _____

9. 79 005 − 32 497 = _____

10. 70 029 − 46 657 = _____

Step 16

1. Two hundred and sixteen thousand and thirty-two subtract one hundred and seventy-two thousand and sixty-one.

   _____

2. Five hundred and six thousand and forty-nine minus three hundred and eleven thousand and fifty-five.

   _____

3. Nine hundred and forty thousand, two hundred and four take away five hundred and eleven thousand and seven.

   _____

Written Calculation — Subtraction

Further practice questions: Steps 17 to 18

Name: _____

Class/Set: _____ Date: _____

Using squared paper for working, work out your answer to each question.
Then write your answer on the line next to the question.

Step 17

1. 443.19 – 66.95 = _____

2. 735.86 – 87.76 = _____

3. 98.35 – 53.84 = _____

4. 316.57 – 78.28 = _____

5. 84.55 – 67.17 = _____

6. 552.47 – 252.97 = _____

7. 355.34 – 56.59 = _____

8. 884.25 – 68.48 = _____

9. 648.65 – 85.36 = _____

10. 763.46 – 52.66 = _____

Step 18

1. 524.7 – 62.97 = _____

2. 355.34 – 5.9 = _____

3. 382.25 – 98.4 = _____

4. 658.65 – 5.536 = _____

5. 44.319 – 6.95 = _____

6. 73.586 – 7.76 = _____

7. 83.58 – 38.4 = _____

8. 321.65 – 77.828 = _____

9. 86.5 – 66.717 = _____

10. 764.6 – 2.66 = _____

From: **Written Calculation: Teacher's Resource Book** by Hilary Koll and Steve Mills (ISBN 978 07217 1300 7). Copyright © Schofield & Sims Ltd, 2015. Published by Schofield & Sims Ltd, Dogley Mill, Fenay Bridge, Huddersfield HD8 0NQ, UK (www.schofieldandsims.co.uk). This page may be photocopied after purchase for use within your school or institution only.

Written Calculation — Subtraction

Problem solving questions

Name: _____

Class/Set: _____ Date: _____

Using squared paper for working, work out your answer to each question.
Then write your answer on the line next to the question.

1 What is 127 subtracted from 875? _____

2 1245 of the 6859 spaces in a car park were empty. How many spaces were taken? _____

3 A TV that cost £1257 is decreased in price by £186. What is the new price? _____

4 Find the difference between 5788 and 2439. _____

5 At a football match there were 738 people. 368 were children. How many were adults? _____

6 Indira had £2443. She spent £1751 of it on a new computer. How much does she have now? _____

7 There are 3104 cabins on a ferry. 1536 of them were occupied. How many cabins were not occupied? _____

8 What is 5735 minus 1978? _____

9 During one week at an airport there were 2024 landings and 1981 take-offs. How many more landings were there than take-offs? _____

10 Some gardeners planted 50037 seeds last year and 83754 this year. How many more seeds did they plant this year than last year? _____

11 Jack's first throw of the javelin went 16.42m. His second throw went 21.63m. How much further did his second throw go? _____

12 How much longer is a piece of wood measuring 8.845m than another piece of wood with a length of 6.75m? _____

From: **Written Calculation: Teacher's Resource Book** by Hilary Koll and Steve Mills (ISBN 978 07217 1300 7). Copyright © Schofield & Sims Ltd, 2015. Published by Schofield & Sims Ltd, Dogley Mill, Fenay Bridge, Huddersfield HD8 0NQ, UK (www.schofieldandsims.co.uk). This page may be photocopied after purchase for use within your school or institution only.

Written Calculation — Multiplication 1

Further practice questions: Steps 1 to 2

Name: _____

Class/Set: _____   Date: _____

Using squared paper for working, work out your answer to each question.
Then write your answer on the line next to the question.

Step 1

1. 13 × 3 = _____
2. 44 × 2 = _____
3. 21 × 4 = _____
4. 32 × 3 = _____
5. 22 × 4 = _____
6. 23 × 3 = _____
7. 31 × 3 = _____
8. 34 × 2 = _____
9. 33 × 3 = _____
10. 24 × 2 = _____

Step 2

1. 24 × 3 = _____
2. 17 × 5 = _____
3. 16 × 3 = _____
4. 17 × 4 = _____
5. 47 × 2 = _____
6. 23 × 4 = _____
7. 27 × 3 = _____
8. 38 × 2 = _____
9. 19 × 3 = _____
10. 18 × 4 = _____

From: **Written Calculation: Teacher's Resource Book** by Hilary Koll and Steve Mills (ISBN 978 07217 1300 7). Copyright © Schofield & Sims Ltd, 2015. Published by Schofield & Sims Ltd, Dogley Mill, Fenay Bridge, Huddersfield HD8 0NQ, UK (www.schofieldandsims.co.uk). This page may be photocopied after purchase for use within your school or institution only.

Written Calculation — Multiplication 1

Further practice questions: Steps 3 to 4

Name: _____

Class/Set: _____ Date: _____

Using squared paper for working, work out your answer to each question.
Then write your answer on the line next to the question.

Step 3

1. 13 × 6 = _____
2. 14 × 7 = _____
3. 16 × 6 = _____
4. 18 × 5 = _____
5. 11 × 9 = _____
6. 15 × 6 = _____
7. 17 × 5 = _____
8. 19 × 4 = _____
9. 12 × 8 = _____
10. 13 × 7 = _____

Step 4

1. 116 × 5 = _____
2. 124 × 4 = _____
3. 113 × 6 = _____
4. 224 × 3 = _____
5. 325 × 3 = _____
6. 214 × 4 = _____
7. 117 × 5 = _____
8. 115 × 6 = _____
9. 113 × 7 = _____
10. 102 × 8 = _____

From: **Written Calculation: Teacher's Resource Book** by Hilary Koll and Steve Mills (ISBN 978 07217 1300 7). Copyright © Schofield & Sims Ltd, 2015. Published by Schofield & Sims Ltd, Dogley Mill, Fenay Bridge, Huddersfield HD8 0NQ, UK (www.schofieldandsims.co.uk). This page may be photocopied after purchase for use within your school or institution only.

Written Calculation — Multiplication 1

Further practice questions: Steps 5 to 6

Name: _____

Class/Set: _____ Date: _____

Using squared paper for working, work out your answer to each question.
Then write your answer on the line next to the question.

Step 5

1. 292 × 3 = _____
2. 131 × 7 = _____
3. 141 × 6 = _____
4. 181 × 5 = _____
5. 242 × 4 = _____
6. 283 × 3 = _____
7. 121 × 8 = _____
8. 151 × 4 = _____
9. 131 × 6 = _____
10. 120 × 8 = _____

Step 6

1. 31 × 7 = _____
2. 61 × 6 = _____
3. 81 × 8 = _____
4. 21 × 9 = _____
5. 72 × 3 = _____
6. 61 × 4 = _____
7. 81 × 6 = _____
8. 91 × 5 = _____
9. 72 × 4 = _____
10. 61 × 8 = _____

From: **Written Calculation: Teacher's Resource Book** by Hilary Koll and Steve Mills (ISBN 978 07217 1300 7). Copyright © Schofield & Sims Ltd, 2015. Published by Schofield & Sims Ltd, Dogley Mill, Fenay Bridge, Huddersfield HD8 0NQ, UK (www.schofieldandsims.co.uk). This page may be photocopied after purchase for use within your school or institution only.

Written Calculation — Multiplication 1

Further practice questions: Steps 7 to 8

Name: _____

Class/Set: _____ Date: _____

Using squared paper for working, work out your answer to each question.
Then write your answer on the line next to the question.

Step 7

1. 78 × 8 = _____
2. 44 × 7 = _____
3. 23 × 6 = _____
4. 82 × 9 = _____
5. 66 × 4 = _____
6. 84 × 3 = _____
7. 52 × 6 = _____
8. 28 × 7 = _____
9. 49 × 8 = _____
10. 55 × 6 = _____

Step 8

1. 122 × 8 = _____
2. 143 × 5 = _____
3. 152 × 6 = _____
4. 138 × 7 = _____
5. 166 × 4 = _____
6. 248 × 3 = _____
7. 145 × 6 = _____
8. 132 × 7 = _____
9. 124 × 8 = _____
10. 145 × 6 = _____

From: **Written Calculation: Teacher's Resource Book** by Hilary Koll and Steve Mills (ISBN 978 07217 1300 7). Copyright © Schofield & Sims Ltd, 2015. Published by Schofield & Sims Ltd, Dogley Mill, Fenay Bridge, Huddersfield HD8 0NQ, UK (www.schofieldandsims.co.uk). This page may be photocopied after purchase for use within your school or institution only.

Written Calculation — Multiplication 1

Further practice questions: Steps 9 to 10

Name: _____

Class/Set: _____ Date: _____

Using squared paper for working, work out your answer to each question.
Then write your answer on the line next to the question.

Step 9

1. 716 × 4 = _____

2. 418 × 3 = _____

3. 205 × 6 = _____

4. 512 × 7 = _____

5. 412 × 8 = _____

6. 315 × 6 = _____

7. 512 × 8 = _____

8. 413 × 7 = _____

9. 312 × 6 = _____

10. 518 × 3 = _____

Step 10

1. 128 × 6 = _____

2. 743 × 3 = _____

3. 941 × 5 = _____

4. 705 × 8 = _____

5. 241 × 7 = _____

6. 852 × 3 = _____

7. 963 × 2 = _____

8. 234 × 4 = _____

9. 306 × 9 = _____

10. 824 × 3 = _____

From: **Written Calculation: Teacher's Resource Book** by Hilary Koll and Steve Mills (ISBN 978 07217 1300 7). Copyright © Schofield & Sims Ltd, 2015. Published by Schofield & Sims Ltd, Dogley Mill, Fenay Bridge, Huddersfield HD8 0NQ, UK (www.schofieldandsims.co.uk). This page may be photocopied after purchase for use within your school or institution only.

Written Calculation — Multiplication 1

Further practice questions: Steps 11 to 12

Name: _____

Class/Set: _____ Date: _____

Using squared paper for working, work out your answer to each question.
Then write your answer on the line next to the question.

Step 11

1. 1427 × 3 = _____

2. 1314 × 7 = _____

3. 1507 × 6 = _____

4. 2481 × 3 = _____

5. 1314 × 4 = _____

6. 1571 × 5 = _____

7. 2636 × 2 = _____

8. 2518 × 3 = _____

9. 1804 × 5 = _____

10. 1241 × 6 = _____

Step 12

1. 5962 × 3 = _____

2. 9970 × 6 = _____

3. 4708 × 5 = _____

4. 8358 × 4 = _____

5. 4437 × 6 = _____

6. 7842 × 7 = _____

7. 8067 × 8 = _____

8. 4428 × 4 = _____

9. 6948 × 9 = _____

10. 7226 × 3 = _____

From: **Written Calculation: Teacher's Resource Book** by Hilary Koll and Steve Mills (ISBN 978 07217 1300 7). Copyright © Schofield & Sims Ltd, 2015. Published by Schofield & Sims Ltd, Dogley Mill, Fenay Bridge, Huddersfield HD8 0NQ, UK (www.schofieldandsims.co.uk). This page may be photocopied after purchase for use within your school or institution only.

Written Calculation

Multiplication 1

Further practice questions: Steps 13 to 14

Name: _____

Class/Set: _____ Date: _____

Using squared paper for working, work out your answer to each question. Then write your answer on the line next to the question.

Step 13

1. 27 058 × 6 = _____

2. 66 305 × 4 = _____

3. 67 401 × 3 = _____

4. 79 805 × 7 = _____

5. 78 047 × 8 = _____

6. 80 603 × 6 = _____

7. 46 059 × 9 = _____

8. 56 036 × 8 = _____

9. 68 034 × 6 = _____

10. 78 026 × 7 = _____

Step 14

1. 852 433 × 8 = _____

2. 466 224 × 7 = _____

3. 523 311 × 5 = _____

4. 634 265 × 3 = _____

5. 781 112 × 2 = _____

6. 685 230 × 3 = _____

7. 635 542 × 4 = _____

8. 633 359 × 6 = _____

9. 7 925 341 × 7 = _____

10. 7 351 225 × 6 = _____

From: **Written Calculation: Teacher's Resource Book** by Hilary Koll and Steve Mills (ISBN 978 07217 1300 7). Copyright © Schofield & Sims Ltd, 2015. Published by Schofield & Sims Ltd, Dogley Mill, Fenay Bridge, Huddersfield HD8 0NQ, UK (www.schofieldandsims.co.uk). This page may be photocopied after purchase for use within your school or institution only.

Written Calculation — Multiplication 1

Further practice questions: Steps 15 to 16

Name: _____

Class/Set: _____   Date: _____

Using squared paper for working, work out your answer to each question.
Then write your answer on the line next to the question.

Step 15

1. 427 × 10 = _____

2. 314 × 20 = _____

3. 507 × 10 = _____

4. 481 × 20 = _____

5. 326 × 20 = _____

6. 571 × 20 = _____

7. 536 × 10 = _____

8. 518 × 20 = _____

9. 804 × 20 = _____

10. 241 × 10 = _____

Step 16

1. 536 × 50 = _____

2. 518 × 80 = _____

3. 804 × 90 = _____

4. 241 × 70 = _____

5. 427 × 30 = _____

6. 314 × 40 = _____

7. 507 × 50 = _____

8. 481 × 60 = _____

9. 314 × 70 = _____

10. 571 × 30 = _____

From: **Written Calculation: Teacher's Resource Book** by Hilary Koll and Steve Mills (ISBN 978 07217 1300 7). Copyright © Schofield & Sims Ltd, 2015. Published by Schofield & Sims Ltd, Dogley Mill, Fenay Bridge, Huddersfield HD8 0NQ, UK (www.schofieldandsims.co.uk). This page may be photocopied after purchase for use within your school or institution only.

Written Calculation — Multiplication 1

Further practice questions: Steps 17 to 18

Name: _____

Class/Set: _____ Date: _____

Using squared paper for working, work out your answer to each question.
Then write your answer on the line next to the question.

Step 17

1. 5356 × 40 = _____
2. 5187 × 80 = _____
3. 8404 × 90 = _____
4. 2641 × 70 = _____
5. 4727 × 30 = _____
6. 3414 × 50 = _____
7. 50 667 × 90 = _____
8. 48 751 × 60 = _____
9. 32 214 × 70 = _____
10. 57 571 × 30 = _____

Step 18

1. 356 × 400 = _____
2. 587 × 800 = _____
3. 1404 × 3000 = _____
4. 641 × 700 = _____
5. 727 × 3000 = _____
6. 414 × 500 = _____
7. 1667 × 900 = _____
8. 751 × 600 = _____
9. 214 × 700 = _____
10. 1571 × 3000 = _____

Written Calculation — Multiplication 1

Problem solving questions

Name: _____

Class/Set: _____ Date: _____

Using squared paper for working, work out your answer to each question. Then write your answer on the line next to the question.

1 A supermarket has 13 bags each containing six apples. How many apples is that altogether? _____

2 If I earn £241 each week, how much do I earn in four weeks? _____

3 A box of matches holds 116 matches. How many matches are in four boxes? _____

4 Find the product of 137 and 7. _____

5 At a football match there were 738 away fans, and three times as many home fans. How many home fans were there? _____

6 What is 4967kg multiplied by five? _____

7 If I earn £2647 each month, how much do I earn in six months? _____

8 Jak earns £26 454 each year for four years. How much does he earn in that time? _____

9 A group of six people won a prize. They each got £4634. How much was the total prize? _____

10 If an aeroplane travels an average of 15 750km per week, how far will it travel in eight weeks? _____

11 Which is greater: 123 456 × 7 or 234 567 × 4? _____

12 Taking a year to be 365 days, how many days are in 50 years? _____

Written Calculation — Multiplication 2

Further practice questions: Steps 1 to 2

Name: _____

Class/Set: _____   Date: _____

Using squared paper for working, work out your answer to each question.
Then write your answer on the line next to the question.

Step 1

1. 427 × 3 = _____

2. 314 × 7 = _____

3. 507 × 6 = _____

4. 4481 × 3 = _____

5. 3314 × 4 = _____

6. 5571 × 5 = _____

7. 7636 × 2 = _____

8. 9518 × 3 = _____

9. 7804 × 5 = _____

10. 4241 × 6 = _____

Step 2

1. 42 × 10 = _____

2. 31 × 20 = _____

3. 547 × 10 = _____

4. 381 × 20 = _____

5. 4314 × 20 = _____

6. 5671 × 20 = _____

7. 5376 × 10 = _____

8. 5818 × 20 = _____

9. 4804 × 20 = _____

10. 6641 × 10 = _____

From: **Written Calculation: Teacher's Resource Book** by Hilary Koll and Steve Mills (ISBN 978 07217 1300 7). Copyright © Schofield & Sims Ltd, 2015. Published by Schofield & Sims Ltd, Dogley Mill, Fenay Bridge, Huddersfield HD8 0NQ, UK (www.schofieldandsims.co.uk). This page may be photocopied after purchase for use within your school or institution only.

Written Calculation   **Multiplication 2**

Further practice questions: Steps 3 to 4

Name: _____

Class/Set: _____ Date: _____

Using squared paper for working, work out your answer to each question.
Then write your answer on the line next to the question.

Step 3

1 103 × 16 = _____

2 104 × 17 = _____

3 306 × 13 = _____

4 213 × 15 = _____

5 102 × 19 = _____

6 214 × 12 = _____

7 33 × 14 = _____

8 532 × 14 = _____

9 202 × 18 = _____

10 43 × 17 = _____

Step 4

1 116 × 15 = _____

2 124 × 14 = _____

3 113 × 16 = _____

4 224 × 13 = _____

5 325 × 13 = _____

6 214 × 14 = _____

7 147 × 15 = _____

8 135 × 16 = _____

9 113 × 17 = _____

10 152 × 18 = _____

From: **Written Calculation: Teacher's Resource Book** by Hilary Koll and Steve Mills (ISBN 978 07217 1300 7). Copyright © Schofield & Sims Ltd, 2015. Published by Schofield & Sims Ltd, Dogley Mill, Fenay Bridge, Huddersfield HD8 0NQ, UK (www.schofieldandsims.co.uk). This page may be photocopied after purchase for use within your school or institution only.

Written Calculation   **Multiplication 2**

Further practice questions: Steps 5 to 6

Name: _____

Class/Set: _____ Date: _____

Using squared paper for working, work out your answer to each question.
Then write your answer on the line next to the question.

Step 5

1. 892 × 15 = _____

2. 731 × 17 = _____

3. 841 × 16 = _____

4. 981 × 15 = _____

5. 642 × 14 = _____

6. 883 × 13 = _____

7. 921 × 18 = _____

8. 751 × 14 = _____

9. 931 × 16 = _____

10. 828 × 18 = _____

Step 6

1. 536 × 50 = _____

2. 518 × 80 = _____

3. 804 × 90 = _____

4. 241 × 70 = _____

5. 427 × 30 = _____

6. 314 × 40 = _____

7. 507 × 50 = _____

8. 481 × 60 = _____

9. 314 × 70 = _____

10. 571 × 30 = _____

From: **Written Calculation: Teacher's Resource Book** by Hilary Koll and Steve Mills (ISBN 978 07217 1300 7). Copyright © Schofield & Sims Ltd, 2015. Published by Schofield & Sims Ltd, Dogley Mill, Fenay Bridge, Huddersfield HD8 0NQ, UK (www.schofieldandsims.co.uk). This page may be photocopied after purchase for use within your school or institution only.

Written Calculation — Multiplication 2

Further practice questions: Steps 7 to 8

Name: _____

Class/Set: _____ Date: _____

Using squared paper for working, work out your answer to each question.
Then write your answer on the line next to the question.

Step 7

1. 72 × 62 = _____

2. 116 × 21 = _____

3. 234 × 38 = _____

4. 61 × 55 = _____

5. 103 × 57 = _____

6. 202 × 44 = _____

7. 71 × 56 = _____

8. 207 × 36 = _____

9. 52 × 28 = _____

10. 34 × 91 = _____

Step 8

1. 78 × 86 = _____

2. 44 × 74 = _____

3. 23 × 62 = _____

4. 107 × 66 = _____

5. 224 × 38 = _____

6. 84 × 39 = _____

7. 58 × 67 = _____

8. 328 × 27 = _____

9. 49 × 48 = _____

10. 115 × 63 = _____

From: **Written Calculation: Teacher's Resource Book** by Hilary Koll and Steve Mills (ISBN 978 07217 1300 7). Copyright © Schofield & Sims Ltd, 2015. Published by Schofield & Sims Ltd, Dogley Mill, Fenay Bridge, Huddersfield HD8 0NQ, UK (www.schofieldandsims.co.uk). This page may be photocopied after purchase for use within your school or institution only.

Written Calculation — Multiplication 2

Further practice questions: Steps 9 to 10

Name: _____

Class/Set: _____   Date: _____

Using squared paper for working, work out your answer to each question.
Then write your answer on the line next to the question.

Step 9

1. 205 × 86 = _____
2. 562 × 97 = _____
3. 716 × 84 = _____
4. 318 × 83 = _____
5. 414 × 78 = _____
6. 755 × 56 = _____
7. 572 × 78 = _____
8. 423 × 87 = _____
9. 342 × 65 = _____
10. 578 × 73 = _____

Step 10

1. 1928 × 66 = _____
2. 7483 × 35 = _____
3. 9641 × 58 = _____
4. 7025 × 82 = _____
5. 2431 × 76 = _____
6. 8542 × 34 = _____
7. 9663 × 23 = _____
8. 2158 × 47 = _____
9. 30 226 × 98 = _____
10. 82 534 × 36 = _____

Written Calculation — Multiplication 2

Further practice questions: Steps 11 to 12

Name: _____

Class/Set: _____ Date: _____

Using squared paper for working, work out your answer to each question. Then write your answer on the line next to the question.

Step 11

1. 278 × 600 = _____
2. 605 × 400 = _____
3. 661 × 300 = _____
4. 795 × 700 = _____
5. 787 × 800 = _____
6. 803 × 600 = _____
7. 459 × 900 = _____
8. 536 × 800 = _____
9. 634 × 600 = _____
10. 726 × 700 = _____

Step 12

1. 278 × 610 _____
2. 605 × 450 = _____
3. 661 × 350 = _____
4. 795 × 740 = _____
5. 787 × 820 = _____
6. 803 × 660 = _____
7. 459 × 910 = _____
8. 536 × 820 = _____
9. 634 × 630 = _____
10. 726 × 780 = _____

From: **Written Calculation: Teacher's Resource Book** by Hilary Koll and Steve Mills (ISBN 978 07217 1300 7). Copyright © Schofield & Sims Ltd, 2015. Published by Schofield & Sims Ltd, Dogley Mill, Fenay Bridge, Huddersfield HD8 0NQ, UK (www.schofieldandsims.co.uk). This page may be photocopied after purchase for use within your school or institution only.

Written Calculation — Multiplication 2

Further practice questions: Steps 13 to 14

Name: _____

Class/Set: _____ Date: _____

Using squared paper for working, work out your answer to each question.
Then write your answer on the line next to the question.

Step 13

1. 278 × 123 = _____
2. 605 × 232 = _____
3. 552 × 251 = _____
4. 125 × 342 = _____
5. 423 × 223 = _____
6. 231 × 562 = _____
7. 124 × 411 = _____
8. 554 × 222 = _____
9. 124 × 133 = _____
10. 245 × 214 = _____

Step 14

1. 852 × 768 = _____
2. 966 × 467 = _____
3. 589 × 578 = _____
4. 676 × 398 = _____
5. 794 × 575 = _____
6. 685 × 876 = _____
7. 685 × 777 = _____
8. 636 × 865 = _____
9. 797 × 976 = _____
10. 788 × 687 = _____

From: **Written Calculation: Teacher's Resource Book** by Hilary Koll and Steve Mills (ISBN 978 07217 1300 7). Copyright © Schofield & Sims Ltd, 2015. Published by Schofield & Sims Ltd, Dogley Mill, Fenay Bridge, Huddersfield HD8 0NQ, UK (www.schofieldandsims.co.uk). This page may be photocopied after purchase for use within your school or institution only.

Written Calculation — Multiplication 2

Further practice questions: Steps 15 to 16

Name: _____

Class/Set: _____ Date: _____

Using squared paper for working, work out your answer to each question.
Then write your answer on the line next to the question.

Step 15

1. $42 \times 0.2 =$ _____

2. $31 \times 0.3 =$ _____

3. $0.34 \times 4 =$ _____

4. $4.1 \times 5 =$ _____

5. $3.4 \times 2 =$ _____

6. $5 \times 3.8 =$ _____

7. $5.6 \times 6 =$ _____

8. $5.8 \times 8 =$ _____

9. $81 \times 0.8 =$ _____

10. $5 \times 4.9 =$ _____

Step 16

1. $3.6 \times 54 =$ _____

2. $18 \times 8.5 =$ _____

3. $64 \times 9.6 =$ _____

4. $4.1 \times 77 =$ _____

5. $2.7 \times 38 =$ _____

6. $1.4 \times 49 =$ _____

7. $57 \times 5.2 =$ _____

8. $81 \times 0.88 =$ _____

9. $0.64 \times 77 =$ _____

10. $0.71 \times 33 =$ _____

Written Calculation — Multiplication 2

Further practice questions: Steps 17 to 18

Name: _____

Class/Set: _____   Date: _____

Using squared paper for working, work out your answer to each question.
Then write your answer on the line next to the question.

Step 17

1. $5.6 \times 4.6 =$ _____

2. $5.7 \times 8.5 =$ _____

3. $8.4 \times 5.7 =$ _____

4. $2.1 \times 6.6 =$ _____

5. $4.7 \times 3.4 =$ _____

6. $3.4 \times 5.3 =$ _____

7. $5.7 \times 9.5 =$ _____

8. $4.1 \times 6.7 =$ _____

9. $3.4 \times 7.6 =$ _____

10. $5.1 \times 0.3 =$ _____

Step 18

1. $3.56 \times 4.8 =$ _____

2. $58.7 \times 8.4 =$ _____

3. $14.4 \times 3.9 =$ _____

4. $6.41 \times 7.4 =$ _____

5. $72.7 \times 0.55 =$ _____

6. $4.14 \times 5.4 =$ _____

7. $1.67 \times 9.7 =$ _____

8. $7.51 \times 6.3 =$ _____

9. $21.4 \times 0.75 =$ _____

10. $15.1 \times 0.45 =$ _____

From: **Written Calculation: Teacher's Resource Book** by Hilary Koll and Steve Mills (ISBN 978 07217 1300 7). Copyright © Schofield & Sims Ltd, 2015. Published by Schofield & Sims Ltd, Dogley Mill, Fenay Bridge, Huddersfield HD8 0NQ, UK (www.schofieldandsims.co.uk). This page may be photocopied after purchase for use within your school or institution only.

Written Calculation — Multiplication 2

Problem solving questions

Name: _____

Class/Set: _____   Date: _____

Using squared paper for working, work out your answer to each question. Then write your answer on the line next to the question.

1. If I have 13 boxes each containing 12 bottles of juice, how many bottles of juice do I have altogether? _____

2. Ping earns £241 each week. How much does she earn in 17 weeks? _____

3. A box of pins holds 116 pins. How many pins are there in 18 boxes? _____

4. Find the product of 136 and 24. _____

5. Taking a year to be 365 days, how many days are in 30 years? _____

6. What is 496g multiplied by 65? _____

7. If an employee earns £2647 each month, how much will this employee earn in 48 months? _____

8. A group of 49 people won the lottery. They each got £4634. What was the total lottery win? _____

9. Which is greater: 456 × 4 or 234 × 8? _____

10. Anuska earns £145 each day for a year. If this year has 365 days, how much will she earn? _____

11. Dan spends £4.37 on bus fare each day. How much does he spend in 25 days? _____

12. A farmer has a field with a length of 654m and a width of 448m. What is the area of the field? _____

From: **Written Calculation: Teacher's Resource Book** by Hilary Koll and Steve Mills (ISBN 978 07217 1300 7). Copyright © Schofield & Sims Ltd, 2015. Published by Schofield & Sims Ltd, Dogley Mill, Fenay Bridge, Huddersfield HD8 0NQ, UK (www.schofieldandsims.co.uk). This page may be photocopied after purchase for use within your school or institution only.

Written Calculation — Division 1

Further practice questions: Steps 1 to 2

Name: _____

Class/Set: _____   Date: _____

Using squared paper for working, work out your answer to each question.
Then write your answer on the line next to the question.

Step 1

1. 63 ÷ 3 = _____
2. 84 ÷ 2 = _____
3. 88 ÷ 4 = _____
4. 93 ÷ 3 = _____
5. 84 ÷ 4 = _____
6. 33 ÷ 3 = _____
7. 69 ÷ 3 = _____
8. 62 ÷ 2 = _____
9. 39 ÷ 3 = _____
10. 46 ÷ 2 = _____

Step 2

1. 963 ÷ 3 = _____
2. 448 ÷ 2 = _____
3. 844 ÷ 4 = _____
4. 669 ÷ 3 = _____
5. 484 ÷ 4 = _____
6. 639 ÷ 3 = _____
7. 309 ÷ 3 = _____
8. 864 ÷ 2 = _____
9. 993 ÷ 3 = _____
10. 648 ÷ 2 = _____

From: **Written Calculation: Teacher's Resource Book** by Hilary Koll and Steve Mills (ISBN 978 07217 1300 7). Copyright © Schofield & Sims Ltd, 2015. Published by Schofield & Sims Ltd, Dogley Mill, Fenay Bridge, Huddersfield HD8 0NQ, UK (www.schofieldandsims.co.uk). This page may be photocopied after purchase for use within your school or institution only.

Written Calculation

Division 1

Further practice questions: Steps 3 to 4

Name: _____

Class/Set: _____   Date: _____

Using squared paper for working, work out your answer to each question.
Then write your answer on the line next to the question.

Step 3

1. 42 ÷ 3 = _____

2. 76 ÷ 2 = _____

3. 92 ÷ 4 = _____

4. 72 ÷ 3 = _____

5. 96 ÷ 4 = _____

6. 75 ÷ 3 = _____

7. 48 ÷ 3 = _____

8. 34 ÷ 2 = _____

9. 45 ÷ 3 = _____

10. 94 ÷ 2 = _____

Step 4

1. 72 ÷ 4 = _____

2. 95 ÷ 5 = _____

3. 56 ÷ 4 = _____

4. 68 ÷ 4 = _____

5. 84 ÷ 6 = _____

6. 90 ÷ 6 = _____

7. 87 ÷ 3 = _____

8. 64 ÷ 4 = _____

9. 57 ÷ 3 = _____

10. 90 ÷ 5 = _____

From: **Written Calculation: Teacher's Resource Book** by Hilary Koll and Steve Mills (ISBN 978 07217 1300 7). Copyright © Schofield & Sims Ltd, 2015. Published by Schofield & Sims Ltd, Dogley Mill, Fenay Bridge, Huddersfield HD8 0NQ, UK (www.schofieldandsims.co.uk). This page may be photocopied after purchase for use within your school or institution only.

Written Calculation — Division 1

Further practice questions: Steps 5 to 6

Name: _____

Class/Set: _____   Date: _____

Using squared paper for working, work out your answer to each question. Then write your answer on the line next to the question.

Step 5

1. 873 ÷ 3 = _____
2. 648 ÷ 4 = _____
3. 579 ÷ 3 = _____
4. 905 ÷ 5 = _____
5. 728 ÷ 4 = _____
6. 955 ÷ 5 = _____
7. 524 ÷ 4 = _____
8. 688 ÷ 4 = _____
9. 846 ÷ 6 = _____
10. 906 ÷ 6 = _____

Step 6

1. 246 ÷ 3 = _____
2. 305 ÷ 5 = _____
3. 279 ÷ 9 = _____
4. 368 ÷ 4 = _____
5. 186 ÷ 2 = _____
6. 546 ÷ 6 = _____
7. 219 ÷ 3 = _____
8. 486 ÷ 6 = _____
9. 248 ÷ 4 = _____
10. 455 ÷ 5 = _____

From: **Written Calculation: Teacher's Resource Book** by Hilary Koll and Steve Mills (ISBN 978 07217 1300 7). Copyright © Schofield & Sims Ltd, 2015. Published by Schofield & Sims Ltd, Dogley Mill, Fenay Bridge, Huddersfield HD8 0NQ, UK (www.schofieldandsims.co.uk). This page may be photocopied after purchase for use within your school or institution only.

Written Calculation — Division 1

Further practice questions: Steps 7 to 8

Name: _____

Class/Set: _____ Date: _____

Using squared paper for working, work out your answer to each question.
Then write your answer on the line next to the question.

Step 7

1. 896 ÷ 8 = _____
2. 784 ÷ 7 = _____
3. 672 ÷ 6 = _____
4. 565 ÷ 5 = _____
5. 860 ÷ 4 = _____
6. 642 ÷ 3 = _____
7. 690 ÷ 6 = _____
8. 791 ÷ 7 = _____
9. 856 ÷ 4 = _____
10. 678 ÷ 6 = _____

Step 8

1. 927 ÷ 3 = _____
2. 624 ÷ 6 = _____
3. 828 ÷ 4 = _____
4. 636 ÷ 6 = _____
5. 728 ÷ 7 = _____
6. 824 ÷ 8 = _____
7. 324 ÷ 3 = _____
8. 816 ÷ 4 = _____
9. 612 ÷ 3 = _____
10. 832 ÷ 8 = _____

From: **Written Calculation: Teacher's Resource Book** by Hilary Koll and Steve Mills (ISBN 978 07217 1300 7). Copyright © Schofield & Sims Ltd, 2015. Published by Schofield & Sims Ltd, Dogley Mill, Fenay Bridge, Huddersfield HD8 0NQ, UK (www.schofieldandsims.co.uk). This page may be photocopied after purchase for use within your school or institution only.

Written Calculation Division 1

Further practice questions: Steps 9 to 10

Name: _____

Class/Set: _____ Date: _____

Using squared paper for working, work out your answer to each question.
Then write your answer on the line next to the question.

Step 9

1. 6978 ÷ 3 = _____

2. 4568 ÷ 4 = _____

3. 8055 ÷ 5 = _____

4. 4866 ÷ 6 = _____

5. 9248 ÷ 4 = _____

6. 5255 ÷ 5 = _____

7. 4206 ÷ 6 = _____

8. 8656 ÷ 2 = _____

9. 3357 ÷ 3 = _____

10. 9807 ÷ 7 = _____

Step 10

1. 525 ÷ 3 = _____

2. 736 ÷ 2 = _____

3. 988 ÷ 4 = _____

4. 486 ÷ 9 = _____

5. 748 ÷ 4 = _____

6. 876 ÷ 6 = _____

7. 558 ÷ 3 = _____

8. 368 ÷ 8 = _____

9. 294 ÷ 7 = _____

10. 956 ÷ 4 = _____

From: **Written Calculation: Teacher's Resource Book** by Hilary Koll and Steve Mills (ISBN 978 07217 1300 7). Copyright © Schofield & Sims Ltd, 2015. Published by Schofield & Sims Ltd, Dogley Mill, Fenay Bridge, Huddersfield HD8 0NQ, UK (www.schofieldandsims.co.uk). This page may be photocopied after purchase for use within your school or institution only.

Written Calculation — Division 1

Further practice questions: Steps 11 to 12

Name: _____

Class/Set: _____ Date: _____

Using squared paper for working, work out your answer to each question.
Then write your answer on the line next to the question.

Step 11

1. 8796 ÷ 6 = _____
2. 3456 ÷ 4 = _____
3. 4075 ÷ 5 = _____
4. 7048 ÷ 8 = _____
5. 4647 ÷ 3 = _____
6. 7968 ÷ 6 = _____
7. 4356 ÷ 4 = _____
8. 9723 ÷ 7 = _____
9. 8778 ÷ 2 = _____
10. 5649 ÷ 3 = _____

Step 12

Give your answers with remainders.

1. 1335 ÷ 4 = _____
2. 436 ÷ 5 = _____
3. 211 ÷ 6 = _____
4. 7537 ÷ 8 = _____
5. 877 ÷ 4 = _____
6. 718 ÷ 7 = _____
7. 9799 ÷ 4 = _____
8. 4444 ÷ 3 = _____
9. 6473 ÷ 6 = _____
10. 4755 ÷ 8 = _____

Written Calculation — Division 1

Further practice questions: Steps 13 to 14

Name: _____

Class/Set: _____ Date: _____

Using squared paper for working, work out your answer to each question.
Then write your answer on the line next to the question.

Step 13
Give your answers with remainders.

1. 15 543 ÷ 3 = _____
2. 44 567 ÷ 5 = _____
3. 22 351 ÷ 4 = _____
4. 32 678 ÷ 7 = _____
5. 24 442 ÷ 9 = _____
6. 26 483 ÷ 6 = _____
7. 31 889 ÷ 3 = _____
8. 35 584 ÷ 8 = _____
9. 33 443 ÷ 3 = _____
10. 28 994 ÷ 7 = _____

Step 14
Give the remainder as a fraction.

1. 1346 ÷ 3 = _____
2. 4475 ÷ 7 = _____
3. 2153 ÷ 8 = _____
4. 3255 ÷ 6 = _____
5. 2279 ÷ 4 = _____
6. 2325 ÷ 9 = _____
7. 3157 ÷ 8 = _____
8. 3445 ÷ 4 = _____
9. 3340 ÷ 7 = _____
10. 2411 ÷ 8 = _____

From: **Written Calculation: Teacher's Resource Book** by Hilary Koll and Steve Mills (ISBN 978 07217 1300 7). Copyright © Schofield & Sims Ltd, 2015. Published by Schofield & Sims Ltd, Dogley Mill, Fenay Bridge, Huddersfield HD8 0NQ, UK (www.schofieldandsims.co.uk). This page may be photocopied after purchase for use within your school or institution only.

Written Calculation — Division 1

Further practice questions: Steps 15 to 16

Name: _____

Class/Set: _____   Date: _____

Using squared paper for working, work out your answer to each question.
Then write your answer on the line next to the question.

Step 15
Give your answer as a decimal.

1. 4561 ÷ 5 = _____

2. 2147 ÷ 5 = _____

3. 5284 ÷ 4 = _____

4. 5636 ÷ 8 = _____

5. 1174 ÷ 5 = _____

6. 3326 ÷ 5 = _____

7. 4860 ÷ 8 = _____

8. 6838 ÷ 4 = _____

9. 7559 ÷ 5 = _____

10. 6765 ÷ 6 = _____

Step 16
Give your answer as a decimal.

1. 5435 ÷ 4 = _____

2. 7657 ÷ 8 = _____

3. 5947 ÷ 4 = _____

4. 7639 ÷ 8 = _____

5. 9075 ÷ 8 = _____

6. 1806 ÷ 8 = _____

7. 7498 ÷ 8 = _____

8. 9161 ÷ 4 = _____

9. 1561 ÷ 8 = _____

10. 7677 ÷ 4 = _____

From: **Written Calculation: Teacher's Resource Book** by Hilary Koll and Steve Mills (ISBN 978 07217 1300 7). Copyright © Schofield & Sims Ltd, 2015. Published by Schofield & Sims Ltd, Dogley Mill, Fenay Bridge, Huddersfield HD8 0NQ, UK (www.schofieldandsims.co.uk). This page may be photocopied after purchase for use within your school or institution only.

Written Calculation — Division 1

Further practice questions: Steps 17 to 18

Name: _____

Class/Set: _____   Date: _____

Using squared paper for working, work out your answer to each question.
Then write your answer on the line next to the question.

Step 17
Give the remainder as a recurring decimal.

1. 137 ÷ 3 = _____
2. 664 ÷ 3 = _____
3. 421 ÷ 9 = _____
4. 344 ÷ 3 = _____
5. 282 ÷ 9 = _____
6. 232 ÷ 6 = _____
7. 317 ÷ 3 = _____
8. 343 ÷ 9 = _____
9. 383 ÷ 3 = _____
10. 242 ÷ 6 = _____

Step 18

1. 6.78 ÷ 3 = _____
2. 4.68 ÷ 4 = _____
3. 8.55 ÷ 5 = _____
4. 4.68 ÷ 6 = _____
5. 9.48 ÷ 4 = _____
6. 1.55 ÷ 5 = _____
7. 4.08 ÷ 6 = _____
8. 8.56 ÷ 2 = _____
9. 3.57 ÷ 3 = _____
10. 8.75 ÷ 7 = _____

Written Calculation — Division 1

Problem solving questions

Name: _____

Class/Set: _____ Date: _____

Using squared paper for working, work out your answer to each question.
Then write your answer on the line next to the question.

1 Divide 488 equally by 4. _____

2 There are 968 fish in eight fish tanks. Each fish tank contains the same number of fish. How many fish are in each tank? _____

3 Six people equally shared £672 in prize money. How much did each person receive? _____

4 If I pay rent of £4740 equally over six months, how much is that each month? _____

5 A plank of wood is 474cm long. It is cut into three equal lengths. How long is each length? _____

6 4528 people go to a rugby match. Exactly one-eighth of them are female. How many are male? _____

7 What is the remainder when 4845 is divided by 6? _____

8 How many weeks is 27 013 days? _____

9 Jenna makes 3548ml of a juice drink for her party. She shares it equally between three large jugs. How much is in each jug? Give your answer with the remainder as a fraction. _____

10 A construction company makes four identical deliveries of sand. The total weight of the sand is 9254kg. How heavy is each delivery? Give your answer as a decimal. _____

11 Which digit recurs in the answer to the question 777 ÷ 9? _____

12 A chef puts 1.86kg of pasta into eight equal piles. How heavy is each pile? _____

From: **Written Calculation: Teacher's Resource Book** by Hilary Koll and Steve Mills (ISBN 978 07217 1300 7). Copyright © Schofield & Sims Ltd, 2015. Published by Schofield & Sims Ltd, Dogley Mill, Fenay Bridge, Huddersfield HD8 0NQ, UK (www.schofieldandsims.co.uk). This page may be photocopied after purchase for use within your school or institution only.

Written Calculation

Division 2

Further practice questions: Steps 1 to 2

Name: _____

Class/Set: _____ Date: _____

Using squared paper for working, work out your answer to each question.
Then write your answer on the line next to the question.

Step 1

1. $196 \div 7 =$ _____

2. $342 \div 9 =$ _____

3. $436 \div 4 =$ _____

4. $729 \div 3 =$ _____

5. $728 \div 7 =$ _____

6. $504 \div 8 =$ _____

7. $456 \div 3 =$ _____

8. $856 \div 4 =$ _____

9. $642 \div 3 =$ _____

10. $832 \div 8 =$ _____

Step 2

Give your answers with remainders.

1. $96\,553 \div 3 =$ _____

2. $44\,433 \div 2 =$ _____

3. $84\,685 \div 4 =$ _____

4. $66\,679 \div 3 =$ _____

5. $48\,477 \div 4 =$ _____

6. $63\,389 \div 3 =$ _____

7. $30\,934 \div 7 =$ _____

8. $56\,431 \div 8 =$ _____

9. $99\,324 \div 9 =$ _____

10. $45\,748 \div 5 =$ _____

From: **Written Calculation: Teacher's Resource Book** by Hilary Koll and Steve Mills (ISBN 978 07217 1300 7). Copyright © Schofield & Sims Ltd, 2015. Published by Schofield & Sims Ltd, Dogley Mill, Fenay Bridge, Huddersfield HD8 0NQ, UK (www.schofieldandsims.co.uk). This page may be photocopied after purchase for use within your school or institution only.

Written Calculation — Division 2

Further practice questions: Steps 3 to 4

Name: _____

Class/Set: _____   Date: _____

Using squared paper for working, work out your answer to each question.
Then write your answer on the line next to the question.

Step 3
Give your answers with remainders.

1. 43 ÷ 3 = _____
2. 77 ÷ 2 = _____
3. 94 ÷ 4 = _____
4. 75 ÷ 3 = _____
5. 97 ÷ 4 = _____
6. 56 ÷ 3 = _____
7. 97 ÷ 6 = _____
8. 85 ÷ 4 = _____
9. 76 ÷ 3 = _____
10. 92 ÷ 7 = _____

Step 4
Give your answers with remainders.

1. 876 ÷ 3 = _____
2. 647 ÷ 4 = _____
3. 578 ÷ 3 = _____
4. 909 ÷ 5 = _____
5. 726 ÷ 4 = _____
6. 954 ÷ 5 = _____
7. 543 ÷ 4 = _____
8. 686 ÷ 4 = _____
9. 848 ÷ 6 = _____
10. 979 ÷ 6 = _____

From: **Written Calculation: Teacher's Resource Book** by Hilary Koll and Steve Mills (ISBN 978 07217 1300 7). Copyright © Schofield & Sims Ltd, 2015. Published by Schofield & Sims Ltd, Dogley Mill, Fenay Bridge, Huddersfield HD8 0NQ, UK (www.schofieldandsims.co.uk). This page may be photocopied after purchase for use within your school or institution only.

Written Calculation — Division 2

Further practice questions: Steps 5 to 6

Name: _____

Class/Set: _____ Date: _____

Using squared paper for working, work out your answer to each question.
Then write your answer on the line next to the question.

Step 5
Give your answers with remainders.

1 8573 ÷ 6 = _____

2 6478 ÷ 5 = _____

3 5279 ÷ 7 = _____

4 6965 ÷ 3 = _____

5 7728 ÷ 8 = _____

6 9555 ÷ 5 = _____

7 5344 ÷ 9 = _____

8 6688 ÷ 6 = _____

9 8446 ÷ 7 = _____

10 9265 ÷ 4 = _____

Step 6
Give your answers with remainders.

1 2115 ÷ 7 = _____

2 2457 ÷ 8 = _____

3 2709 ÷ 9 = _____

4 3008 ÷ 6 = _____

5 1446 ÷ 7 = _____

6 4842 ÷ 6 = _____

7 2121 ÷ 3 = _____

8 4086 ÷ 4 = _____

9 2129 ÷ 7 = _____

10 3642 ÷ 6 = _____

From: **Written Calculation: Teacher's Resource Book** by Hilary Koll and Steve Mills (ISBN 978 07217 1300 7). Copyright © Schofield & Sims Ltd, 2015. Published by Schofield & Sims Ltd, Dogley Mill, Fenay Bridge, Huddersfield HD8 0NQ, UK (www.schofieldandsims.co.uk). This page may be photocopied after purchase for use within your school or institution only.

Written Calculation — Division 2

Further practice questions: Steps 7 to 8

Name: _____

Class/Set: _____ Date: _____

Using squared paper for working, work out your answer to each question.
Then write your answer on the line next to the question.

Step 7
Give your answers with remainders.

1. 896 ÷ 11 = _____
2. 784 ÷ 11 = _____
3. 672 ÷ 11 = _____
4. 565 ÷ 11 = _____
5. 860 ÷ 11 = _____
6. 642 ÷ 11 = _____
7. 690 ÷ 11 = _____
8. 791 ÷ 11 = _____
9. 856 ÷ 11 = _____
10. 678 ÷ 11 = _____

Step 8
Give your answers with remainders.

1. 9927 ÷ 11 = _____
2. 6704 ÷ 11 = _____
3. 8908 ÷ 11 = _____
4. 6636 ÷ 11 = _____
5. 7808 ÷ 11 = _____
6. 8824 ÷ 11 = _____
7. 3324 ÷ 11 = _____
8. 8816 ÷ 11 = _____
9. 6702 ÷ 11 = _____
10. 8852 ÷ 11 = _____

From: **Written Calculation: Teacher's Resource Book** by Hilary Koll and Steve Mills (ISBN 978 07217 1300 7). Copyright © Schofield & Sims Ltd, 2015. Published by Schofield & Sims Ltd, Dogley Mill, Fenay Bridge, Huddersfield HD8 0NQ, UK (www.schofieldandsims.co.uk). This page may be photocopied after purchase for use within your school or institution only.

Written Calculation

Division 2

Further practice questions: Steps 9 to 10

Name: _____

Class/Set: _____   Date: _____

Using squared paper for working, work out your answer to each question.
Then write your answer on the line next to the question.

Step 9
Give your answers with remainders.

1. 6978 ÷ 12 = _____

2. 4568 ÷ 12 = _____

3. 8055 ÷ 12 = _____

4. 4206 ÷ 12 = _____

5. 4866 ÷ 12 = _____

6. 9248 ÷ 12 = _____

7. 5255 ÷ 12 = _____

8. 8656 ÷ 12 = _____

9. 3357 ÷ 12 = _____

10. 9807 ÷ 12 = _____

Step 10
Give your answers with remainders.

1. 5325 ÷ 13 = _____

2. 7356 ÷ 13 = _____

3. 9887 ÷ 13 = _____

4. 4836 ÷ 13 = _____

5. 7448 ÷ 13 = _____

6. 8766 ÷ 13 = _____

7. 5528 ÷ 13 = _____

8. 3608 ÷ 13 = _____

9. 2924 ÷ 13 = _____

10. 9516 ÷ 13 = _____

From: **Written Calculation: Teacher's Resource Book** by Hilary Koll and Steve Mills (ISBN 978 07217 1300 7). Copyright © Schofield & Sims Ltd, 2015. Published by Schofield & Sims Ltd, Dogley Mill, Fenay Bridge, Huddersfield HD8 0NQ, UK (www.schofieldandsims.co.uk). This page may be photocopied after purchase for use within your school or institution only.

Written Calculation — Division 2

Further practice questions: Steps 11 to 12

Name: _____

Class/Set: _____ Date: _____

Using squared paper for working, work out your answer to each question.
Then write your answer on the line next to the question.

Step 11
Give your answers with remainders.

1. 7968 ÷ 16 = _____

2. 4356 ÷ 14 = _____

3. 9723 ÷ 16 = _____

4. 8778 ÷ 15 = _____

5. 8796 ÷ 14 = _____

6. 3456 ÷ 15 = _____

7. 4075 ÷ 16 = _____

8. 7048 ÷ 14 = _____

9. 4647 ÷ 15 = _____

10. 5649 ÷ 14 = _____

Step 12
Give your answers with remainders.

1. 1335 ÷ 17 = _____

2. 1436 ÷ 18 = _____

3. 1211 ÷ 19 = _____

4. 1537 ÷ 17 = _____

5. 1777 ÷ 18 = _____

6. 1718 ÷ 19 = _____

7. 1399 ÷ 17 = _____

8. 1444 ÷ 18 = _____

9. 1473 ÷ 19 = _____

10. 1155 ÷ 17 = _____

From: **Written Calculation: Teacher's Resource Book** by Hilary Koll and Steve Mills (ISBN 978 07217 1300 7). Copyright © Schofield & Sims Ltd, 2015. Published by Schofield & Sims Ltd, Dogley Mill, Fenay Bridge, Huddersfield HD8 0NQ, UK (www.schofieldandsims.co.uk). This page may be photocopied after purchase for use within your school or institution only.

Written Calculation — Division 2

Further practice questions: Steps 13 to 14

Name: _____

Class/Set: _____ Date: _____

Using squared paper for working, work out your answer to each question.
Then write your answer on the line next to the question.

Step 13
Give your answers with remainders.

1. 1554 ÷ 13 = _____
2. 4457 ÷ 11 = _____
3. 2251 ÷ 16 = _____
4. 3678 ÷ 18 = _____
5. 4442 ÷ 14 = _____
6. 6483 ÷ 19 = _____
7. 3889 ÷ 15 = _____
8. 3554 ÷ 11 = _____
9. 3343 ÷ 12 = _____
10. 2894 ÷ 19 = _____

Step 14
Give the remainder as a fraction.

1. 1346 ÷ 13 = _____
2. 4475 ÷ 17 = _____
3. 2153 ÷ 18 = _____
4. 3255 ÷ 16 = _____
5. 2279 ÷ 14 = _____
6. 2325 ÷ 19 = _____
7. 3157 ÷ 18 = _____
8. 3445 ÷ 14 = _____
9. 3340 ÷ 17 = _____
10. 2411 ÷ 18 = _____

From: **Written Calculation: Teacher's Resource Book** by Hilary Koll and Steve Mills (ISBN 978 07217 1300 7). Copyright © Schofield & Sims Ltd, 2015. Published by Schofield & Sims Ltd, Dogley Mill, Fenay Bridge, Huddersfield HD8 0NQ, UK (www.schofieldandsims.co.uk). This page may be photocopied after purchase for use within your school or institution only.

Written Calculation — Division 2

Further practice questions: Steps 15 to 16

Name: _____

Class/Set: _____   Date: _____

Using squared paper for working, work out your answer to each question.
Then write your answer on the line next to the question.

Step 15
Give the remainder as a fraction.

1 4561 ÷ 25 = _____

2 2147 ÷ 22 = _____

3 5284 ÷ 21 = _____

4 5636 ÷ 23 = _____

5 1174 ÷ 26 = _____

6 3326 ÷ 27 = _____

7 4860 ÷ 28 = _____

8 6838 ÷ 24 = _____

9 7559 ÷ 29 = _____

10 6765 ÷ 26 = _____

Step 16
Give the remainder as a fraction.

1 5435 ÷ 34 = _____

2 7657 ÷ 48 = _____

3 5947 ÷ 44 = _____

4 7639 ÷ 28 = _____

5 9075 ÷ 48 = _____

6 1806 ÷ 58 = _____

7 7498 ÷ 32 = _____

8 9161 ÷ 41 = _____

9 1561 ÷ 36 = _____

10 7677 ÷ 37 = _____

From: **Written Calculation: Teacher's Resource Book** by Hilary Koll and Steve Mills (ISBN 978 07217 1300 7). Copyright © Schofield & Sims Ltd, 2015. Published by Schofield & Sims Ltd, Dogley Mill, Fenay Bridge, Huddersfield HD8 0NQ, UK (www.schofieldandsims.co.uk). This page may be photocopied after purchase for use within your school or institution only.

Written Calculation — Division 2

Further practice questions: Steps 17 to 18

Name: _____

Class/Set: _____ Date: _____

Using squared paper for working, work out your answer to each question.
Then write your answer on the line next to the question.

Step 17
Give your answer as a decimal.

1. 715 ÷ 26 = _____

2. 560 ÷ 32 = _____

3. 999 ÷ 45 = _____

4. 483 ÷ 35 = _____

5. 182 ÷ 28 = _____

6. 923 ÷ 65 = _____

7. 629 ÷ 34 = _____

8. 775 ÷ 62 = _____

9. 861 ÷ 35 = _____

10. 775 ÷ 62 = _____

Step 18
Give your answer as a decimal.

1. 175 ÷ 28 = _____

2. 240 ÷ 64 = _____

3. 949 ÷ 52 = _____

4. 371 ÷ 28 = _____

5. 474 ÷ 24 = _____

6. 901 ÷ 68 = _____

7. 882 ÷ 72 = _____

8. 675 ÷ 36 = _____

9. 583 ÷ 44 = _____

10. 792 ÷ 32 = _____

From: **Written Calculation: Teacher's Resource Book** by Hilary Koll and Steve Mills (ISBN 978 07217 1300 7). Copyright © Schofield & Sims Ltd, 2015. Published by Schofield & Sims Ltd, Dogley Mill, Fenay Bridge, Huddersfield HD8 0NQ, UK (www.schofieldandsims.co.uk). This page may be photocopied after purchase for use within your school or institution only.

Written Calculation — Division 2

Problem solving questions

Name: _____

Class/Set: _____ Date: _____

Using squared paper for working, work out your answer to each question.
Then write your answer on the line next to the question.

1 How many weeks is 27412 days? (Use long division.) _____

2 Divide 488 by 11 and give your answer with a remainder. _____

3 Work out my monthly salary if I earn £26412 in a year. _____

4 Thirteen people equally shared £6864 in prize money. How much did they each get? _____

5 624 sunbeds are arranged in rows of 16 on the beach. How many rows of sunbeds are there? _____

6 4004 people go to a theme park. Exactly one-seventh of them are children. How many children are there? _____

7 What is the remainder when 4836 is divided by 16? _____

8 There are 24 hours in a day. How many days is 8760 hours? _____

9 If I raised £5356 in a year for charity, how much is that on average each week, taking a year to be 52 weeks? _____

10 If the length of a 609m wall is divided equally into 42 sections, what is the length of each section? _____

11 There are 28 days in February. Govi was given £133 for his paper round in February. How much is that on average each day? _____

12 How much is £833 shared equally between 49 people? _____

From: **Written Calculation: Teacher's Resource Book** by Hilary Koll and Steve Mills (ISBN 978 07217 1300 7). Copyright © Schofield & Sims Ltd, 2015. Published by Schofield & Sims Ltd, Dogley Mill, Fenay Bridge, Huddersfield HD8 0NQ, UK (www.schofieldandsims.co.uk). This page may be photocopied after purchase for use within your school or institution only.

Answers

Written Calculation — Addition: Answers

Addition: Further practice answers

	Step 1	Step 2	Step 3	Step 4	Step 5
1	87	889	391	915	1162
2	78	886	671	716	1316
3	98	397	992	928	1328
4	88	668	862	628	1285
5	99	996	991	863	1350
6	89	887	850	747	1317
7	76	895	971	718	1292
8	89	999	893	839	1163
9	94	984	870	718	1747
10	88	897	896	969	1495

	Step 6	Step 7	Step 8	Step 9	Step 10
1	961	6334	634	5734	10 184
2	926	6129	804	8184	10 234
3	1483	8174	411	7134	10 334
4	1767	6764	732	6732	15 562
5	1564	8937	772	6772	14 732
6	856	9147	932	8872	10 172
7	1156	6723	1311	8305	10 305
8	1669	7439	843	9237	10 237
9	1349	8926	1311	9151	16 553
10	2019	9905	1041	7441	14 441

From: **Written Calculation: Teacher's Resource Book** by Hilary Koll and Steve Mills (ISBN 978 07217 1300 7). Copyright © Schofield & Sims Ltd, 2015. Published by Schofield & Sims Ltd, Dogley Mill, Fenay Bridge, Huddersfield HD8 0NQ, UK (www.schofieldandsims.co.uk). This page may be photocopied after purchase for use within your school or institution only.

Written Calculation — Addition: Answers

Addition: Further practice answers continued

Step 11
1. 11 214
2. 16 062
3. 13 422
4. 11 004
5. 15 132
6. 12 124
7. 11 122
8. 16 413
9. 15 141
10. 13 432

Step 12
1. 17 250
2. 7598
3. 18 642
4. 14 207
5. 14 156
6. 20 529
7. 18 372
8. 13 871
9. 11 256
10. 16 552

Step 13
1. 73 742
2. 160 362
3. 109 993
4. 151 282
5. 106 014
6. 120 544
7. 133 912
8. 111 193
9. 164 073
10. 151 401

Step 14
1. 49 425
2. 39 300
3. 79 608
4. 29 899
5. 95 048

Step 15
1. 588 093
2. 1 217 104
3. 1 151 211

Step 16
1. 63.4
2. 80.4
3. 41.1
4. 142.2
5. 277.2
6. 93.2
7. 761.1
8. 384.3
9. 1251.1
10. 1024.1

Step 17
1. 510.14
2. 823.62
3. 452.19
4. 1094.85
5. 751.72
6. 1205.44
7. 1111.93
8. 852.73
9. 734.01
10. 816.12

Step 18
1. 587.67
2. 361.24
3. 880.65
4. 664.186
5. 51.269
6. 81.346
7. 421.98
8. 399.478
9. 153.217
10. 767.26

Addition: Problem solving answers

1. 695
2. 5658
3. £1443
4. 1168
5. 2003 (AD)
6. 11 698
7. 94 441
8. 9724
9. 41.1m
10. £60.43
11. 883.62
12. £672 529

From: **Written Calculation: Teacher's Resource Book** by Hilary Koll and Steve Mills (ISBN 978 07217 1300 7). Copyright © Schofield & Sims Ltd, 2015. Published by Schofield & Sims Ltd, Dogley Mill, Fenay Bridge, Huddersfield HD8 0NQ, UK (www.schofieldandsims.co.uk). This page may be photocopied after purchase for use within your school or institution only.

Written Calculation — Subtraction: Answers

Subtraction: Further practice answers

	Step 1	Step 2	Step 3	Step 4	Step 5
1	35	324	128	191	97
2	43	222	347	374	374
3	11	412	127	284	309
4	35	315	628	280	227
5	21	134	249	496	244
6	31	311	237	163	393
7	54	621	347	371	616
8	61	122	357	492	673
9	32	224	117	353	607
10	41	493	459	761	159

	Step 6	Step 7	Step 8	Step 9	Step 10
1	1924	3768	568	2834	2033
2	2904	2546	276	3266	7308
3	2940	2818	469	4245	2784
4	3305	3724	198	2981	3474
5	3781	3948	348	3840	4117
6	3602	3759	478	2059	2051
7	4601	2739	189	4771	3260
8	4501	4527	489	2695	3782
9	2635	1754	135	1165	4177
10	3701	5707	699	2673	4171

From: **Written Calculation: Teacher's Resource Book** by Hilary Koll and Steve Mills (ISBN 978 07217 1300 7). Copyright © Schofield & Sims Ltd, 2015. Published by Schofield & Sims Ltd, Dogley Mill, Fenay Bridge, Huddersfield HD8 0NQ, UK (www.schofieldandsims.co.uk). This page may be photocopied after purchase for use within your school or institution only.

Written Calculation — Subtraction: Answers

Subtraction: Further practice answers continued

Step 11	Step 12	Step 13	Step 14	Step 15
1 28 648	1 26 665	1 13 782	1 44 869	1 44 439
2 68 283	2 56 374	2 24 177	2 32 659	2 26 459
3 4445	3 25 675	3 42 033	3 30 446	3 28 138
4 13 918	4 37 636	4 47 308	4 27 539	4 27 119
5 52 413	5 41 674	5 33 474	5 63 345	5 55 295
6 15 304	6 23 465	6 49 117	6 19 783	6 19 265
7 20 406	7 62 385	7 32 784	7 15 673	7 12 133
8 36 364	8 61 654	8 34 171	8 33 691	8 30 161
9 58 304	9 40 279	9 32 051	9 46 734	9 46 508
10 28 291	10 41 353	10 63 260	10 26 868	10 23 372

Step 16	Step 17	Step 18
1 43 971	1 376.24	1 461.73
2 194 994	2 648.1	2 349.44
3 429 197	3 44.51	3 283.85
	4 238.29	4 653.114
	5 17.38	5 37.369
	6 299.50	6 65.826
	7 298.75	7 45.18
	8 815.77	8 243.822
	9 563.29	9 19.783
	10 710.80	10 761.94

Subtraction: Problem solving answers

1 748
2 5614
3 £1071
4 3349
5 370
6 £692
7 1568
8 3757
9 43
10 33 717
11 5.21m
12 2.095m

From: **Written Calculation: Teacher's Resource Book** by Hilary Koll and Steve Mills (ISBN 978 07217 1300 7). Copyright © Schofield & Sims Ltd, 2015. Published by Schofield & Sims Ltd, Dogley Mill, Fenay Bridge, Huddersfield HD8 0NQ, UK (www.schofieldandsims.co.uk). This page may be photocopied after purchase for use within your school or institution only.

Written Calculation — Multiplication 1: Answers

Multiplication 1: Further practice answers

	Step 1	Step 2	Step 3	Step 4	Step 5
1	39	72	78	580	876
2	88	85	98	496	917
3	84	48	96	678	846
4	96	68	90	672	905
5	88	94	99	975	968
6	69	92	90	856	849
7	93	81	85	585	968
8	68	76	76	690	604
9	99	57	96	791	786
10	48	72	91	816	960

	Step 6	Step 7	Step 8	Step 9	Step 10
1	217	624	976	2864	768
2	366	308	715	1254	2229
3	648	138	912	1230	4705
4	189	738	966	3584	5640
5	216	264	664	3296	1687
6	244	252	744	1890	2556
7	486	312	870	4096	1926
8	455	196	924	2891	936
9	288	392	992	1872	2754
10	488	330	870	1554	2472

From: **Written Calculation: Teacher's Resource Book** by Hilary Koll and Steve Mills (ISBN 978 07217 1300 7). Copyright © Schofield & Sims Ltd, 2015. Published by Schofield & Sims Ltd, Dogley Mill, Fenay Bridge, Huddersfield HD8 0NQ, UK (www.schofieldandsims.co.uk). This page may be photocopied after purchase for use within your school or institution only.

Written Calculation — Multiplication 1: Answers

Multiplication 1: Further practice answers continued

	Step 11	Step 12	Step 13	Step 14	Step 15
1	4281	17 886	162 348	6 819 464	4270
2	9198	59 820	265 220	3 263 568	6280
3	9042	23 540	202 203	2 616 555	5070
4	7443	33 432	558 635	1 902 795	9620
5	5256	26 622	624 376	1 562 224	6520
6	7855	54 894	483 618	2 055 690	11 420
7	5272	64 536	414 531	2 542 168	5360
8	7554	17 712	448 288	3 800 154	10 360
9	9020	62 532	408 204	55 477 387	16 080
10	7446	21 678	546 182	44 107 350	2410

	Step 16	Step 17	Step 18
1	26 800	214 240	142 400
2	41 440	414 960	469 600
3	72 360	756 360	4 212 000
4	16 870	184 870	448 700
5	12 810	141 810	2 181 000
6	12 560	170 700	207 000
7	25 350	4 560 030	1 500 300
8	28 860	2 925 060	450 600
9	21 980	2 254 980	149 800
10	17 130	1 727 130	4 713 000

Multiplication 1: Problem solving answers

1. 78
2. £964
3. 464
4. 959
5. 2214
6. 24 835 kg
7. £15 882
8. £105 816
9. £27 804
10. 126 000 km
11. 234 567 × 4 = 938 268
12. 18 250 days

From: **Written Calculation: Teacher's Resource Book** by Hilary Koll and Steve Mills (ISBN 978 07217 1300 7). Copyright © Schofield & Sims Ltd, 2015. Published by Schofield & Sims Ltd, Dogley Mill, Fenay Bridge, Huddersfield HD8 0NQ, UK (www.schofieldandsims.co.uk). This page may be photocopied after purchase for use within your school or institution only.

Written Calculation — Multiplication 2: Answers

Multiplication 2: Further practice answers

	Step 1	Step 2	Step 3	Step 4	Step 5
1	1281	420	1648	1740	13 380
2	2198	620	1768	1736	12 427
3	3042	5470	3978	1808	13 456
4	13 443	7620	3195	2912	14 715
5	13 256	86 280	1938	4225	8988
6	27 855	113 420	2568	2996	11 479
7	15 272	53 760	462	2205	16 578
8	28 554	116 360	7448	2160	10 514
9	39 020	96 080	3636	1921	14 896
10	25 446	66 410	731	2736	14 904

	Step 6	Step 7	Step 8	Step 9	Step 10
1	26 800	4464	6708	17 630	127 248
2	41 440	2436	3256	54 514	261 905
3	72 360	8892	1426	60 144	559 178
4	16 870	3355	7062	26 394	576 050
5	12 810	5871	8512	32 292	184 756
6	12 560	8888	3276	42 280	290 428
7	25 350	3976	3886	44 616	222 249
8	28 860	7452	8856	36 801	101 426
9	21 980	1456	2352	22 230	2 962 148
10	17 130	3094	7245	42 194	2 971 224

From: **Written Calculation: Teacher's Resource Book** by Hilary Koll and Steve Mills (ISBN 978 07217 1300 7). Copyright © Schofield & Sims Ltd, 2015. Published by Schofield & Sims Ltd, Dogley Mill, Fenay Bridge, Huddersfield HD8 0NQ, UK (www.schofieldandsims.co.uk). This page may be photocopied after purchase for use within your school or institution only.

Written Calculation — Multiplication 2: Answers

> **Multiplication 2: Further practice answers** continued

Step 11	Step 12	Step 13	Step 14	Step 15
1. 166 800	1. 169 580	1. 34 194	1. 654 336	1. 8.4
2. 242 000	2. 272 250	2. 140 360	2. 451 122	2. 9.3
3. 198 300	3. 231 350	3. 138 552	3. 340 442	3. 1.36
4. 556 500	4. 588 300	4. 42 750	4. 269 048	4. 20.5
5. 629 600	5. 645 340	5. 94 329	5. 456 550	5. 6.8
6. 481 800	6. 529 980	6. 129 822	6. 600 060	6. 19
7. 413 100	7. 417 690	7. 50 964	7. 532 245	7. 33.6
8. 428 800	8. 439 520	8. 122 988	8. 550 140	8. 46.4
9. 380 400	9. 399 420	9. 16 492	9. 777 872	9. 64.8
10. 508 200	10. 566 280	10. 52 430	10. 541 356	10. 24.5

Step 16	Step 17	Step 18
1. 194.4	1. 25.76	1. 17.088
2. 153	2. 48.45	2. 493.08
3. 614.4	3. 47.88	3. 56.16
4. 315.7	4. 13.86	4. 47.434
5. 102.6	5. 15.98	5. 39.985
6. 68.6	6. 18.02	6. 22.356
7. 296.4	7. 54.15	7. 16.199
8. 71.28	8. 27.47	8. 47.313
9. 49.28	9. 25.84	9. 16.05
10. 23.43	10. 1.53	10. 6.795

Multiplication 2: Problem solving answers

1. 156
2. £4097
3. 2088
4. 3264
5. 10 950 days
6. 32 240 g
7. £127 056
8. £227 066
9. 234 × 8 = 1872
10. £52 925
11. £109.25
12. 292 972 m²

From: **Written Calculation: Teacher's Resource Book** by Hilary Koll and Steve Mills (ISBN 978 07217 1300 7). Copyright © Schofield & Sims Ltd, 2015. Published by Schofield & Sims Ltd, Dogley Mill, Fenay Bridge, Huddersfield HD8 0NQ, UK (www.schofieldandsims.co.uk). This page may be photocopied after purchase for use within your school or institution only.

Written Calculation — Division 1: Answers

Division 1: Further practice answers

	Step 1	Step 2	Step 3	Step 4	Step 5
1	21	321	14	18	291
2	42	224	38	19	162
3	22	211	23	14	193
4	31	223	24	17	181
5	21	121	24	14	182
6	11	213	25	15	191
7	23	103	16	29	131
8	31	432	17	16	172
9	13	331	15	19	141
10	23	324	47	18	151

	Step 6	Step 7	Step 8	Step 9	Step 10
1	82	112	309	2326	175
2	61	112	104	1142	368
3	31	112	207	1611	247
4	92	113	106	811	54
5	93	215	104	2312	187
6	91	214	103	1051	146
7	73	115	108	701	186
8	81	113	204	4328	46
9	62	214	204	1119	42
10	91	113	104	1401	239

From: **Written Calculation: Teacher's Resource Book** by Hilary Koll and Steve Mills (ISBN 978 07217 1300 7). Copyright © Schofield & Sims Ltd, 2015. Published by Schofield & Sims Ltd, Dogley Mill, Fenay Bridge, Huddersfield HD8 0NQ, UK (www.schofieldandsims.co.uk). This page may be photocopied after purchase for use within your school or institution only.

Written Calculation — Division 1: Answers

Division 1: Further practice answers continued

	Step 11	Step 12	Step 13	Step 14	Step 15
1	1466	333 r3	5181	$448\frac{2}{3}$	912.2
2	864	87 r1	8913 r2	$639\frac{2}{7}$	429.4
3	815	35 r1	5587 r3	$269\frac{1}{8}$	1321
4	881	942 r1	4668 r2	$542\frac{1}{2}$	704.5
5	1549	219 r1	2715 r7	$569\frac{3}{4}$	234.8
6	1328	102 r4	4413 r5	$258\frac{1}{3}$	665.2
7	1089	2449 r3	10 629 r2	$394\frac{5}{8}$	607.5
8	1389	1481 r1	4448	$861\frac{1}{4}$	1709.5
9	4389	1078 r5	11 147 r2	$477\frac{1}{7}$	1511.8
10	1883	594 r3	4142	$301\frac{3}{8}$	1127.5

	Step 16	Step 17	Step 18
1	1358.75	45.$\dot{6}$	2.2600
2	957.125	221.$\dot{3}$	1.1700
3	1486.75	46.$\dot{7}$	1.7100
4	954.875	114.$\dot{6}$	0.7800
5	1134.375	31.$\dot{3}$	2.3700
6	225.75	38.$\dot{6}$	0.3100
7	937.25	105.$\dot{6}$	0.6800
8	2290.25	38.$\dot{1}$	4.2800
9	195.125	127.$\dot{6}$	1.1900
10	1919.25	40.$\dot{3}$	1.2500

Division 1: Problem solving answers

1. 122
2. 121
3. £112
4. £790
5. 158cm
6. 3962
7. 3
8. 3859 weeks
9. $1182\frac{2}{3}$ ml
10. 2313.5kg
11. 3
12. 232.5g (or 0.2325kg)

From: **Written Calculation: Teacher's Resource Book** by Hilary Koll and Steve Mills (ISBN 978 07217 1300 7). Copyright © Schofield & Sims Ltd, 2015. Published by Schofield & Sims Ltd, Dogley Mill, Fenay Bridge, Huddersfield HD8 0NQ, UK (www.schofieldandsims.co.uk). This page may be photocopied after purchase for use within your school or institution only.

Written Calculation — Division 2: Answers

Division 2: Further practice answers

Step 1
1. 28
2. 38
3. 109
4. 243
5. 104
6. 63
7. 152
8. 214
9. 214
10. 104

Step 2
1. 32 184 r1
2. 22 216 r1
3. 21 171 r1
4. 22 226 r1
5. 12 119 r1
6. 21 129 r2
7. 4419 r1
8. 7053 r7
9. 11036
10. 9149 r3

Step 3
1. 14 r1
2. 38 r1
3. 23 r2
4. 25
5. 24 r1
6. 18 r2
7. 16 r1
8. 21 r1
9. 25 r1
10. 13 r1

Step 4
1. 292
2. 161 r3
3. 192 r2
4. 181 r4
5. 181 r2
6. 190 r4
7. 135 r3
8. 171 r2
9. 141 r2
10. 163 r1

Step 5
1. 1428 r5
2. 1295 r3
3. 754 r1
4. 2321 r2
5. 966
6. 1911
7. 593 r7
8. 1114 r4
9. 1206 r4
10. 2316 r1

Step 6
1. 302 r1
2. 307 r1
3. 301
4. 501 r2
5. 206 r4
6. 807
7. 707
8. 1021 r2
9. 304 r1
10. 607

Step 7
1. 81 r5
2. 71 r3
3. 61 r1
4. 51 r4
5. 78 r2
6. 58 r4
7. 62 r8
8. 71 r10
9. 77 r9
10. 61 r7

Step 8
1. 902 r5
2. 609 r5
3. 809 r9
4. 603 r3
5. 709 r9
6. 802 r2
7. 302 r2
8. 801 r5
9. 609 r3
10. 804 r8

Step 9
1. 581 r6
2. 380 r8
3. 671 r3
4. 350 r6
5. 405 r6
6. 770 r8
7. 437 r11
8. 721 r4
9. 279 r9
10. 817 r3

Step 10
1. 409 r8
2. 565 r11
3. 760 r7
4. 372
5. 572 r12
6. 674 r4
7. 425 r3
8. 277 r7
9. 224 r12
10. 732

From: **Written Calculation: Teacher's Resource Book** by Hilary Koll and Steve Mills (ISBN 978 07217 1300 7). Copyright © Schofield & Sims Ltd, 2015. Published by Schofield & Sims Ltd, Dogley Mill, Fenay Bridge, Huddersfield HD8 0NQ, UK (www.schofieldandsims.co.uk). This page may be photocopied after purchase for use within your school or institution only.

Written Calculation — Division 2: Answers

Division 2: Further practice answers continued

Step 11
1. 498
2. 311 r2
3. 607 r11
4. 585 r3
5. 628 r4
6. 230 r6
7. 254 r11
8. 503 r6
9. 309 r12
10. 403 r7

Step 12
1. 78 r9
2. 79 r14
3. 63 r14
4. 90 r7
5. 98 r13
6. 90 r8
7. 82 r5
8. 80 r4
9. 77 r10
10. 67 r16

Step 13
1. 119 r7
2. 405 r2
3. 140 r11
4. 204 r6
5. 317 r4
6. 341 r4
7. 259 r4
8. 323 r1
9. 278 r7
10. 152 r6

Step 14
1. $103\frac{7}{13}$
2. $263\frac{4}{17}$
3. $119\frac{11}{18}$
4. $203\frac{7}{16}$
5. $162\frac{11}{14}$
6. $122\frac{7}{19}$
7. $175\frac{7}{18}$
8. $246\frac{1}{14}$
9. $196\frac{8}{17}$
10. $133\frac{17}{18}$

Step 15
1. $182\frac{11}{25}$
2. $97\frac{13}{22}$
3. $251\frac{13}{21}$
4. $245\frac{1}{23}$
5. $45\frac{2}{13}$ (or $\frac{4}{26}$)
6. $123\frac{5}{27}$
7. $173\frac{4}{7}$ (or $\frac{16}{28}$)
8. $284\frac{11}{12}$ (or $\frac{22}{24}$)
9. $260\frac{19}{29}$
10. $260\frac{5}{26}$

Step 16
1. $159\frac{29}{34}$
2. $159\frac{25}{48}$
3. $135\frac{7}{44}$
4. $272\frac{23}{28}$
5. $189\frac{1}{16}$ (or $\frac{3}{48}$)
6. $31\frac{4}{29}$ (or $\frac{8}{58}$)
7. $234\frac{5}{16}$ (or $\frac{10}{32}$)
8. $223\frac{18}{41}$
9. $43\frac{13}{36}$
10. $207\frac{18}{37}$

Step 17
1. 27.5
2. 17.5
3. 22.2
4. 13.8
5. 6.5
6. 14.2
7. 18.5
8. 12.5
9. 24.6
10. 12.5

Step 18
1. 6.25
2. 3.75
3. 18.25
4. 13.25
5. 19.75
6. 13.25
7. 12.25
8. 18.75
9. 13.25
10. 24.75

Division 2: Problem solving answers
1. 3916 weeks
2. 44 r4
3. £2201
4. £528
5. 39
6. 572
7. 4
8. 365 days
9. £103
10. 14.5m
11. £4.75
12. £17